THE COWBOY AND HIS HORSE

THE COWBOY
AND HIS HORSE

By SYDNEY E. FLETCHER

WITH AN INTRODUCTION BY
JOSEPH HENRY JACKSON

Publishers   GROSSET & DUNLAP   New York

ACKNOWLEDGMENTS

The author and the publishers wish to express appreciation to Bantam Books, Inc., for permission to use the music and words for "Sweet Betsy from Pike" and "Night-Herding Song" from A TREASURY OF FOLK SONGS by Sylvia and John Kolb, 1948, and to George W. Saunders for permission to use "Did You Ever Do the Square?" from THE TRAIL DRIVERS OF TEXAS, edited by John Marvin Hunter, Cokesbury Press, 1926.

DEDICATED
TO ALL COWBOYS
PAST AND PRESENT

CONTENTS

INTRODUCTION IX

1. RIDE 'EM, COWBOY! 13

2. AN EARLY TRAIL DRIVE 26

3. COWBOY FUN 29

4. AFTER THE RAILROADS CAME 34

5. ALONG THE TRAIL 43

6. STAMPEDE! 55

7. COWBOYS IN CALIFORNIA 60

8. SPRING ROUNDUP 69

9. BRANDS AND BRANDING 73

10. BIG SPREADS IN TEXAS 87

11. THE COWBOY'S EQUIPMENT 90

12. COWBOY RIDING 108

VII

13. RANGE RIDERS 114

14. COWBOY DANCE 120

15. THE OLD AND THE NEW 123

16. RODEOS—WEST AND EAST 128

GLOSSARY OF COWBOY TERMS

BIBLIOGRAPHY

INDEX

INTRODUCTION

THE AMERICAN COWBOY, as everybody knows, is a very special kind of character. He has been a very special character for a good many years, too. Cowboys have been around a long time, and all that time they have been an important part of the Western picture.

Now, of course, there are different kinds of cowboys. There is the movie cowboy, and the television cowboy, for example, and there is the cowboy in a lot of "Western" yarns. These cowboys lead a life principally of fighting Indians and rescuing beautiful maidens, and they always seem to dress as if they were slicked up for Saturday night in town, even when they're in the middle of a roundup and ought to be dust from head to foot.

The real, working cowboy is something else. And that's the cowboy you will find in this book, both in text and in pictures.

Where did the cowboy come from in the beginning? How did he happen to select the kind of hat he wears, or the type of boots you find him using? How about his spurs, his chaps, the handkerchief around his neck? What about the Western saddle and how it came to be designed the way it is?

This is the kind of question Mr. Sydney Fletcher answers—this and a lot more, such as how the cowboy originated, how cowboy lingo grew up and came into use, what the cowboy's horse is like and what it must be able to do, and why. In fact, this is barely a beginning. Mr. Fletcher knows the cowboy from spurs to Stetson, and he knows

The Cowboy and His Horse

the cowboy's job and the cowboy's horse just as well. You'll go a long way before you find anything better, in either words or pictures, about cattle or about horses, or about the men who handle them both.

But this still is only part of the book.

The cowboy has to earn a living, and he has done this for upwards of a hundred years in America. What is his job like? What must a top hand know, and how good has he got to be?

You will find these things too in Mr. Fletcher's book, along with a lot else about the good points of the job and some of the headaches.

For example, the chapter "An Early Trail Drive" gives you the picture of the old days when the Chisholm Trail was a busy stretch, one way and another, and Mr. Fletcher has made that chapter a completely authentic story. As you will see also, there are chapters on branding, on cowboy riding and some of the special things you have to know in that direction; on what happens during the spring round-up, and on how the old-time cowboy (and the cowboy today) would go about having a good time. You'll even find the story of the rodeo, how it began, and what today's rodeos are like, West and East.

To my mind, though, the really great thing about Mr. Fletcher's text and pictures is the fact that they're right. Every time you get the real thing, and no guff. To get some idea of this, you might look at Chapter 11 and see how carefully Mr. Fletcher shows the types of spurs, kinds of saddle and so on.

But after all, this is true of the book throughout. When you have a man who knows the cowboy at first-hand and knows how to write and draw both—well, my recommendation is to get right along past this comment and into the book itself. If you have even the faintest interest in the cowboy you've got a real treat coming. And along with the pleasure you will get out of it all, you'll suddenly find you're learning a lot that perhaps you didn't know about the great West and the cattle business that first made the West tick.

JOSEPH HENRY JACKSON

THE COWBOY AND HIS HORSE

Every bucking bronc "swallows," or lowers, his head to get started. The saddle bronc rider in a rodeo has only one rein and must always keep one hand up in the air. With every rider goes a pick-up man who catches the bronc when the rider dismounts or is thrown.

CHAPTER 1

RIDE 'EM
COWBOY!

IMAGINE YOU'RE SITTING RIGHT NOW in the grandstand at
—say, the Custer County Rodeo in Broken Bow, Nebraska. The saddle
bronc riding contest is on. A cowboy gets ready to drop down into the
saddle on a rearing, snorting bronc in the chute at the end of the arena.

"And now, out of gate five, comes the Horseshoe Bar entry," the
announcer bellows, "Bud Wyatt, riding Sun Dog, the meanest, fight-
ingest piece of hoss flesh north of the Colorado line!"

The gate opens, and out plunges a thousand pounds of four-legged
dynamite. Bud Wyatt holds one hand free and hooks both spurs high
on the bronco's quivering shoulders. The duel between horse and rider
begins. Sun Dog is mad and cunning and stubborn. He is determined
to get rid of the uninvited load on his back.

Horseshoe Bar Brand.

13

The Cowboy
and
His Horse

When a bucking bronc turns in the air and makes a half-circle, cowboys say he swaps ends.

About all Bud has to fight back with is his courage, his sense of balance and timing — and his brains.

Sun Dog, head down between his legs, humps his back. Then he squeals shrilly and suddenly becomes an exploding powder mine, earthquake and tornado, all in one. He's up in the air and then lands with a terrific stiff-legged jolt. In the next leap he corkscrews so suddenly you think even the saddle will break loose. Then up go his hindquarters fast enough to throw almost anything off over his head. And now fancy switches on all these tricks, and then some.

Bronc riders are tough, but it's hard to see how any human body can take the punishment Sun Dog is giving to Bud Wyatt. It seems like hours, and Sun Dog has tried every trick in the bag. The only thing he hasn't done yet is roll over on top of Bud to get rid of him. Broncs sometimes do. They even get so blind, fighting mad that they will run head-on into a fence and kill themselves just to throw a rider.

Suddenly a horn sounds and the ride is over. It's only been a minute, and by sticking on Sun Dog for sixty seconds Bud Wyatt has won the chance to ride in the finals tomorrow. An old cowboy saying goes: "There ain't a hoss that can't be rode; there ain't a man that can't be throwed."

As you relax and take a swig of soda pop, you're secretly glad it was the cowpoke from the Horseshoe Bar ranch, and not you, who was forking that bronc!

Next comes the bulldogging contest, in which cowboys wrestle steers. Then the calf roping. From the way cowboys work, you might think that they have been swinging lariats as long as there have been animals to swing them at. But there's more to the story than that, and it's not always just what you might expect. So, before we go on to rodeos and the cowboys who take part in them, let's ride a fast trail through the old West and see what's what.

COWBOY WAYS IN OLD MEXICO

Before you go far, you'll see one thing clear enough. A lot of cowboy words and a lot of cowboy ways come from old Mexico. That's only natural because the Spaniards brought the first horses and cattle to America, when they took over Mexico more than four hundred years ago.

Cortez, who led the Spanish conquest of Mexico, brought the first cattle to America. His brand was three crosses.

One of the first real ranches in Mexico used this brand. Most Mexican brands were very complicated.

Part of the early Mexican Cow's Head brand showing the outline of a cow's head on the left.

15

The Cowboy and His Horse

The first Spanish horses that crossed the Atlantic Ocean were war horses, and there were just sixteen of them. Spanish gentlemen, called *caballeros,* rode them into battle wearing heavy armor and spurs. Spurs were an age-old symbol of the horseman, but it didn't take long before anyone who did much riding found they were useful as well as important looking. Cowboys still wear spurs, even when they don't have to. They are proud of them.

The horses and the caballeros together were a kind of secret weapon for the Spanish invaders. Indians in Mexico had never seen such a sight before, and they thought horse and rider were all one animal. When you see a huge, strange, armed creature charging down on you, your

16

At first Mexican vaqueros tried to herd cattle with a long pole, or pike. Soon found they needed a better tool.

first idea is to get out of the way. And that's just what the Indians did. Before long Mexico had been conquered.

Some of the first sixteen horses lived through the campaign, and more came later. All of them were descendants of the Arab horses the Moors had brought to Spain a long time before that.

When the Spaniards decided to stay in Mexico, they figured it was easier to get meat from cattle than to go out and kill wild game. So they brought in long-horned, yellow-hided cows and bulls from Andalusia in southern Spain. These small, rangy beasts could cover a lot of ground. And there was a lot of ground to cover in Mexico. There was fine grass for grazing, too, and a warm climate. The herds grew larger and larger, and they kept spreading farther and farther north.

JOSE AND HIS REATA

As the cattle came, Spanish cowherds called *vaqueros* came along to take care of them. At first, the vaqueros tried to handle the animals the way they did in the old country, but it didn't work. Herding was different in these vast open spaces. The vaqueros couldn't even use their favorite tool which was a sharp-pointed pole or pike. In Spanish pastures and on narrow roads a pike could make a herd mosey along. But it wasn't the handiest thing to carry around when you had to ride herd, day after day.

The vaqueros did manage to catch some of the critters and burn a brand on them with a hot iron, but a good many got away. So one day some vaquero, maybe his name was José, got the idea of lassoing calves with a noose on the end of a long rope. His scheme worked, and before long all vaqueros were using ropes, or *reatas*, which we call lariats today.

Some other vaquero, maybe an hombre named Juan, decided there was no reason why a cantankerous animal should pull the reata out of his hands. The running rope burned his skin, for one thing, and besides there was always the chance he would lose the rope for good.

Ride 'em Cowboy!

Some pikes had three points. Others had only one.

17

The Cowboy and His Horse

Juan figured that all he had to do was to wrap the rope around something solid. So he had a small post or horn built into the pommel of his saddle. After he had caught an animal, he made a few quick turns of the rope around the saddle horn, and the trick was done.

The Spanish words for taking a turn with a rope are *dar la vuelta.* English-speaking cowboys shortened this to dally, and they still use the word today.

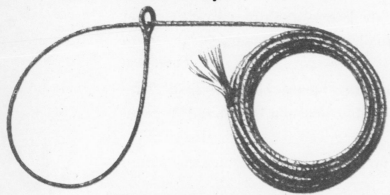

Vaqueros made ropes of braided rawhide. They called them reatas, from which we get the word lariat. The small eye through which the rope passes to make the loop is the honda.

As the longhorns kept moving farther north, of course the vaqueros followed. Cattle and men crossed the Rio Grande river into Texas, which was then still part of Mexico. Huge ranches grew up, where vaqueros worked with the herds.

Over the years the first Texans, together with all other Mexicans, grew restless under the rule of far-away Spain. In 1821 they declared their independence from Spain, just as the English colonists farther north had broken away from England in 1776.

THE OPENING UP OF TEXAS

This Mexican revolution had a lot to do with cowboys in the United States. It helped to make them the way they are today, and here is why.

Right after the revolution, the new Mexican government invited anybody and everybody to settle in Texas. Many people from the United States, particularly southerners, moved in. These newcomers had the independence fever, too, and only fifteen years later Texas declared its own independence from Mexico.

There were some people who fought the idea of a separate Texas. Many of them were rich landowners, and when they lost, they fled back across the Rio Grande to Mexico, leaving the country and the cattle wide open for the newcomers from the United States. Anybody who wanted longhorns could have them for the taking.

Another thing the Mexicans left behind was their cow-sense — everything they had taught the new settlers, and even their Negro slaves, about handling cattle. The vaquero's saddle, quirt, bit, bridle, spurs, and lariat were in Texas to stay, and so were many of the vaqueros themselves. They had only been peons under the rich Mexican landowners, but they were right there showing the settlers how to use the tools of their trade.

But there was one thing nobody had to teach these new Texans, and that was how to ride a horse. They had grown up in the saddle. Some had even ridden the tough little marsh tackies, which also were descendants of Spanish settlers' horses, running wild in the swampy palmetto lands of Florida.

COWHUNTERS IN THE EARLY DAYS

After ten years as a Republic, Texas joined the United States. This made sense to the Texans because many of them had come from the United States. And they hoped also that by joining they would make more money from the millions of longhorns which now roamed wild on the prairies. But there hadn't been much money in cattle before 1845. Railroads hadn't been built to carry them to places where people could buy them for meat. This meant the cattle were good only for their hides and for the tallow which could be melted down from their fat.

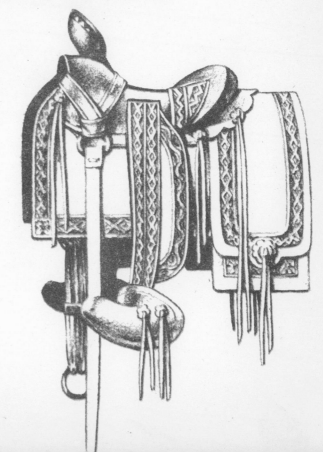

Ride 'em Cowboy!

This early Mexican saddle shows the post (now called a saddle horn) around which a vaquero could turn or tie his rope. The saddle was thickly padded and was much bigger and clumsier than the stock saddle which cowboys use today.

19

The Cowboy and His Horse

The markets for these things were in towns along the coast. So, instead of killing the cattle on the range, the Texans made them carry their own hides and tallow to market. Young settlers, with their Mexican tools and skills, became cowhunters.

In the earliest days they just chased the longhorns day and night when there was a full moon, until the cattle were tired out and easily corralled in pens. The cowhunters themselves had extra horses ready at certain points along the way. Riders would shift their saddles to fresh mounts, just as Pony Express riders did later. Then off they would go again after the tiring cattle. But really big drives hadn't started yet.

Danger and hardship were everyday affairs to the young cowhunters. They were self-reliant, hard-muscled and tough. In the saddle, or in the leather, as cowboys often say nowadays, they rode relaxed—loose and easy.

Some of them wore the frontiersman's jacket and leggins made of buckskin. Others had clothes made of homespun cloth. But all knew the value of a vaquero's broad-brimmed sombrero. It was a combination sun-shade, umbrella and drinking cup. And in winter, when its broad brim was held down with a handkerchief, it also served as ear muffs.

Shoes and boot makers were a long time catching up with the needs

Ride 'em Cowboy!

Early cowhunters in Texas chased cattle day and night to tire the critters and make them easier to handle. Sometimes in order to "spook," or stir up a herd, a cowhunter could gallop along dragging a buffalo hide.

The Cowboy and His Horse

of the cowhunters on the frontier. So they copied the footwear of Indians and wore moccasins.

As they rode out on the range, cowhunters sometimes met Indians who were on the warpath because they couldn't see why they should give up their hunting grounds. And a man had to look out for rattlesnakes too — both the kind that crawled on the ground, and the two-legged kind that rode horseback. So a cowhunter always went armed. He was likely to carry a long-barreled muzzle-loading Kentucky rifle,

Most of the cowhunters were young. People got to calling them cowboys, and the name has stuck ever since.

22

a Colt pistol, and a Bowie knife. This famous knife was not only a weapon which could be thrown with deadly accuracy or used in a fight. It was a tool the cowhunter needed in skinning and cutting up a steer when he wanted a good juicy steak. Because his guns were not mere decorations, he was often a crack shot. He had to be.

THE MUSTANG—AMERICA'S FIRST COWHORSE

These first North American cowboys rode tough, wiry mustangs, captured from bands of wild horses, which were called *mestiños* in Spanish.

Once trained, or broke, a mustang made a good cowhorse. He had a short stride and could start fast and stop almost in his tracks. This short stride made him very good at covering rough ground, and he had more endurance than any other breed of horse at that time. Without their mustangs Texas cowboys could never have covered so much territory with cattle on the run.

This knife, with a nine-inch blade and point sharpened on both edges, was first made from a file by a Negro slave in Texas. Colonel James Bowie of Mississippi saw the knife and liked it so much he had copies made, and the knife was given his name.

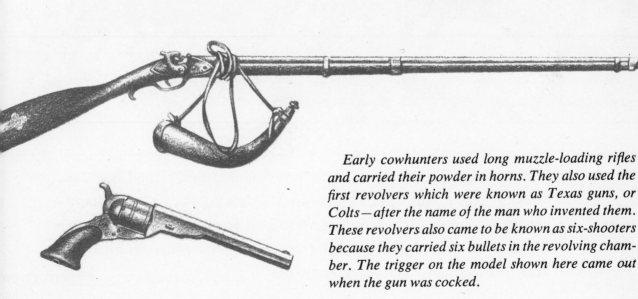

Early cowhunters used long muzzle-loading rifles and carried their powder in horns. They also used the first revolvers which were known as Texas guns, or Colts—after the name of the man who invented them. These revolvers also came to be known as six-shooters because they carried six bullets in the revolving chamber. The trigger on the model shown here came out when the gun was cocked.

23

The Cowboy and His Horse

Mustangs had another use, too. They were a lot easier to sell for money than longhorns were. As pioneers pushed west in Nebraska and Kansas, and later across the Rocky Mountains, they needed good tough horses that had been broken to the saddle. Texans were the ones who knew how to catch and break wild horses.

Some cowboys became mustangers, and they carried their knowledge of horses all over the West, because the mustangs roamed farther north than the longhorns did. And with the horses went the Texas saddle.

Bands of mustangs, descended from Spanish horses, roamed throughout the West. These wild horses were small, weighing only six or seven hundred pounds. A cow horse today weighs about a thousand pounds.

Pioneers found it cheaper to buy the mustangs that had been broken than to get horses from stock farms back east, and many a mustang went to California with the Gold Rush in 1849. Still others climbed all over the steep Colorado mountains when another gold rush started there ten years later.

With the inrush of gold miners, Denver grew quickly, and everybody wanted fresh meat. Texas cowboys knew where to get it. They began driving herds all the way from Texas to Denver. These still weren't the famous big cattle drives, though. They started ten years later when the railroads came. But meantime, cowboys tried moving longhorns overland to places as far away as Chicago and California.

Ride 'em Cowboy!

CHAPTER 2

AN EARLY TRAIL DRIVE

LONG DRIVES WERE TOUGH PROPOSITIONS AT BEST. They had to go through hostile Indian country. Sometimes it was hard to find water for the cattle. Thieves often made off with whole herds. And one more thing. It took some time to learn the best ways of herding cattle over long distances.

Early in the game, cowboys learned that one steer in a herd was often a natural leader. He was kept at the head of the herd and was called a lead steer, or bell ox.

26

Here's a story about a fifteen-hundred-mile drive to California, told by Lem Tolliver, who rode for the old Rafter C Ranch in Palo Pinto County, Texas:

"We was trailing a herd of beefs to Californy by way of the old Californy-Arizona Trail. We made it, but 'twasn't none of our doing.

It was because we had a smart old bell-ox, name of Cochise, along.

"Well, suh, the going was all to the good crossing New Mexico into Arizony, but from then on 'twas plenty tough. First off, we lost us twenty-two head of cows and four horses when we swum the Colorado at Topock, above Needles. Quicksand shore can be bad medicine after a flash flood. Seemed like the critters bogged down

27

Horned toads are among the few animals that can live in the desert.

faster than 'twould take a grass fire in a high wind to scorch a feather. There wasn't nothing we could do, so we had to ride off and leave 'em. Sand ketched one of the crew, too — a kid named Pete Jennings. Nobody knowed it happened till him and his hoss turned up missing. All we found was his hat.

"Then we started crossing the Colorado desert, and afore we knowed it we had a dry drive on our hands. The water we figured on was just dried-up mud holes. We roughed it out but it was hotter than the handle of a frying pan with the heat waves a-coming up offen the ground like smoke. The third day the herd was strung out more than a mile, the big steers in front and the old dogies and cripples trailing, their tongues lolling out a foot. Most of them had already went blind. And we wasn't seeing so good either. That night there was a purty good moon, so we shoved the critters along best we could.

"HE LET OUT A BELLER AND HEADED SOUTHWEST"

Come the morning of the fourth day, so help me if'n that Cochise-steer don't sniff the wind a couple of times like a bird dog, let out a beller and head southwest. We knowed he smelled water, and the rest of the cows knowed it too. Well, that old bell-ox kept a-bellering and a-walking and the hull herd follered the sound. The trail boss put three hands in front to hold the leaders back while the rest of us brung up the rear. It was a good five miles, and it took us four hours to get there. Then the herd made a run for it, and cows, hosses and men all went off in the drink together. The water was so bad a feller had to chew it afore he could swaller it, but we drank it jest the same.

"Well, suh, we lay over two days resting up, and when we tallied out the herd every cow was counted. After that we climbed the San Bernardino Mountains, hit the Coast, and wintered snug as a coon in a holler stump between Santa Ana and Los Angeles."

At early cowboy dances, girls, or "calicos," were scarce. Cow-
boys had to take their place. They wore white handkerchiefs on
their arms and were said to be "heifer-branded."

CHAPTER 3

COWBOY FUN

LEM TOLLIVER'S DRIVE was only one of the tough experiences
the early cowboys had. But they had fun, too. They sang, for one
thing. Sometimes at night they sang around camp fires on the open
range, and they often sang alone at night as they rode around and
around a herd, keeping the cattle from straying away in the darkness.
Cowboys have always believed that singing soothes the cattle so they
won't get excited and run off in a bunch.

29

The Cowboy and His Horse

In the early days, before cowboys had made up their own songs, they sang songs they remembered from their childhood. Many of them had come from parts of the South where everyone knew some of the old ballads which their ancestors had brought with them from England and Scotland. Others came from the prankish life of frontier towns. On a starry night in Texas there was many a young rider singing a tune that had been a favorite throughout the West — and which remains a very popular folk song today, *Sweet Betsy from Pike*. You will find the words and music for this song over on page 32.

They had dances now and then, and they naturally asked girls to come when they could. But often there were no girls within a hundred miles when the cowboys felt like having a good time. So they danced anyway. Half the cow waddies, as they often called themselves, put handkerchiefs around their arms and pretended they were the ladies in the dance. With some old hand playing a fiddle, they would often go on all night. If you think the waddies in the picture are being impolite, you're wrong. They always kept their spurs and hats on as they danced.

Like the songs, most of the dances came from the South. Later, as people moved into the West from New England, they brought their own dances. Many of the square dances people still dance were favorites in Texas a hundred years ago.

Cowboys celebrated in a big way whenever they went to town, which wasn't often. Sometimes these celebrations began with shooting for fun, and ended with shooting in earnest.

Besides singing, and dancing and celebrating in town, cowboys

After months of lonely riding on the range or wi
30 *a cattle drive, cowboys let off steam when they g*
to town. Galloping into Abilene, or Dodge City
any cow town, on pay day they sometimes shot
their six-shooters just to announce they were rea
for a good time.

had fun in another way which has made them famous. They were proud of their skill with rope and horse, and often when there was time off from work, they had contests with each other. Waddies from one outfit challenged waddies from another, to see which one had the best bronc rider or roper or the fastest pony. Cowboys enjoyed these sports immensely, but they never boxed or wrestled. They played, as they worked, on horseback, and when they fought they did it with guns.

From this pleasure cowboys took in using the tools of their trade came the rodeo, which is the word the Mexican vaqueros used for a roundup. Of course, these early riding and roping contests were a long way from the fancy big-time rodeos of today. But they had the makings of a sport that is really exciting and much to the cowboy's liking.

Cowboy Fun

SWEET BETSY FROM PIKE

Oh, don't you re - mem - ber sweet Bet - sy from Pike,

Who crossed the big moun - tains with her lov - er Ike,

With two yoke of ox - en, a large yal - ler dog,

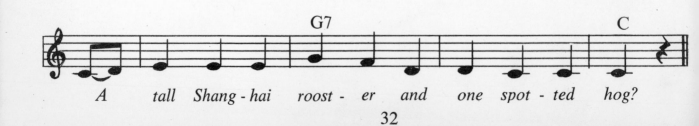

A tall Shang - hai roost - er and one spot - ted hog?

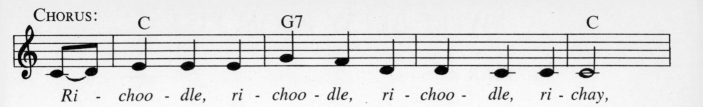

Ri - choo - dle, ri - choo - dle, ri - choo - dle, ri - chay,

Ri - choo - dle, ri - choo - dle, ri - choo - dle, ri - chay.

One evening quite early they camped on the Platte,
'Twas near by the road on a green shady flat,
Where Betsy, sore-footed, lay down to repose—
With wonder Ike gazed on that Pike County rose.
CHORUS

The Shanghai ran off, and their cattle all died;
That morning the last piece of bacon was fried;
Poor Ike was discouraged and Betsy got mad,
The dog drooped his tail and looked wondrously sad.
CHORUS

They soon reached the desert where Betsy gave out,
And down in the sand she lay rolling about;
While Ike, half distracted, looked on with surprise,
Saying, "Betsy, get up, you'll get sand in your eyes."
CHORUS

Sweet Betsy got up in a great deal of pain,
Declared she'd go back to Pike County again;
But Ike gave a sigh, and they fondly embraced,
And they travelled along with his arm round her waist.
CHORUS

The Injuns came down in a wild yelling horde,
And Betsy was skeered they would scalp her adored;
Behind the front wagon wheel Betsy did crawl,
And there she fought the Injuns with musket and ball.
CHORUS

Long Ike and sweet Betsy attended a dance;
Ike wore a pair of his Pike County pants;
Sweet Betsy was dressed up in ribbons and rings;
Says Ike, "You're an angel, but where are your wings?"
CHORUS

A miner said, "Betsy, will you dance with me?"
"I will, you old hoss, if you don't make too free;
But don't dance me hard; do you want to know why?
Doggone ye, I'm chock-full of strong alkali!"
CHORUS

The Cowboy and His Horse

along the Chisholm Trail. This trail soon became known as *the* cow trail up from the Lone Star State.

The Chisholm was a good natural route through the flat grassy areas in unmapped Indian Territory, and here's how it was laid out: an old trader, Jesse Chisholm, did it in 1865. He had no intention of marking a trail for others to follow. He just started for Kansas,

As Jesse Chisholm traveled north, his heavily loaded wagons left deep ruts in the rain-soaked prairie — and other traders following his tracks pounded down what came to be called the Chisholm Trail.

by the best route he knew — and he knew them all. As he went, he ran into rain storms, and his wagons, heavily loaded with buffalo hides, left deep ruts in the prairie grass.

It was easy for other traders to follow these wagon tracks, and some of them did, making more tracks. It wasn't long before cattle drives followed them, too, and ranches sent their hands off in search of markets. Cowboys discovered from experience that the Chisholm

36

Trail was a good one, and within three years of the time the wheels of the old trader's wagons had left their marks in the sod, the Trail Drive Era had begun.

Businessmen who bought cattle and who owned railroads were as eager as the ranchers to find a way of getting the longhorns to market. By 1866 they saw to it that the railroad poked down closer to Texas, as far as Abilene, Kansas. There they built stockyards to hold the cattle until they could be loaded onto railroad cars.

In no time, the whole United States became interested in the "cow country." There were more and more people in the East. They wanted more and more meat. Texas had the cowboys, cow ponies and cattle, and now the railroads saw to it that the cattle could get to market. Although other towns soon began to ship cattle, Abilene remained important for years.

Some cowhands, called "bull nurses," rode in the caboose of each cattle train in the early days. Their job was to keep cattle on their feet so they wouldn't be trampled to death or smothered by each other. Whenever the train stopped, the bull nurse would poke a spike-topped punch pole through the slats of the cattle car to prod any steer which was lying down. The terms "cowpoke" and "cow puncher" came from this part of the cowboy's work.

The Cowboy and His Horse

Abilene was not much of a place by modern standards, but it was paradise to the hard-riding cowboy who had been two or three months driving a herd up from Texas. On the way, he spent eighteen hours a day in the saddle, more often than not. When he arrived, he wanted something else to do for a change, and he had money to spend. Not much to be sure — in the early drives a cowboy got only about fifteen dollars a month. Later he was paid maybe fifty a month. If he was very expert — a top hand — he got sixty. But there was no way to spend money except in town, so the cowboy spent it — fast.

First off, he was likely to get a shave and a haircut. There were no barber shops along the Chisholm Trail, and a waddie always arrived looking "wild and woolly." In fact, if he was asked where he'd come from he'd probably say, "I come up the Chisholm Trail with the wild and woolly buffalo." In those days huge buffalo herds were migrating north about the same time as the cattle drives.

After the haircut he got some new clothes in one of the four or five one-story, frame dry-goods and clothing stores along the dusty main street. He might get a new wide-brimmed, flat-crowned beaver hat, a fancy shirt, a pair of high-heeled boots, and maybe a vest which he knew he would never button, "for fear of taking cold." And he might get something for his horse, a new bridle, or bit, or pair of tapaderos with designs stamped in the leather. After that he "did" the town with what money he had left.

CUTTING UP IN A FRONTIER TOWN

The average cowboy was a young fellow, and he cut up plenty, meaning no harm to anyone. Sometimes he rode right into stores, and even shot his Colt at mirrors or anything else that was handy. As a rule the celebrating was harmless horseplay. The young, good-natured Texans just let off steam like any bunch of kids. Before they knew it most of them had parted with their hard-earned money. So they saddled up for the long ride back to Texas.

38

Before long railroads reached out to other prairie towns, and cattle were shipped from them, as well as from Wichita and Abilene. At the same time big herds of longhorns were driven to new ranches which were growing up all over the West. And the cowboys on these

After the Railroads Came

At the end of a long drive nothing felt so good as a "store bought" haircut and a hot bath in the tub kept in the back of each frontier town barber shop.

northern ranches were Texans, or had learned their trade from Texans. Texas was the teacher of all cowboys in the West and Northwest.

The Texas cow pony spread all over, too. Something like a million horses moved north at the same time as the big cattle drives. Some came

The Cowboy and His Horse

in separate horse drives. Others came as part of remudas with cattle drives and were sold in the cow town at the end of a drive.

The big herds of longhorns, perhaps ten million altogether, moved north all through the 1870's, and the Texas cowboys learned every trick of handling cattle on the trail.

They knew what to do and when to do it. Here's what it would have been like on a big Texas outfit while a trail herd was being shaped up in the 1870's.

SPRING ROUNDUP ON AN OLD-TIME RANCH

The work begins in March at the first sign of spring — "comin' new grass," the cowboys call it. By starting early, the cattle will have plenty to eat all along the trail, and plenty of time to reach the railroad before cold weather sets in.

It takes a couple of weeks to round up the thousands of longhorns from all over the spread. Wearing homemade bull-hide chaps, some cowboys, called circle hands, ride far out on the range and then work toward each other. They look for yellowbacks everywhere, and chase them out of arroyos and thick brush where many of them hide. They

Circle riders often had a tough job rounding up single steers who hid away in the thickets. Cowboys called these steers "windies" because both cowpoke and horse were likely to be out of wind after chasing one.

bring small bunches together and then shove them along toward a big open space where there is soon a bawling, shuffling herd, throwing up a haze of dust.

At first you wonder whether anything makes sense from here on, but the hands know what they are about, and they work together smoothly.

As circle riders bring in each new bunch, cutters ride in among them. It is the cutters' job to separate, or cut out, the good beef cattle from all the others that have been rounded up. They can tell at a glance whether steers are four years old, or older, and these are the ones they are after. Cowboys call them fours-an'-up.

A skillful cutter can edge the beeves off to one side, a dozen or so at a time, and turn them over to other cowboys who drive them into the holding herd. The young calves are cut out too, for they have to be branded. All this takes wits and speed and a well-trained cow pony that can dodge around in the midst of the racketing longhorns.

After the Railroads Came

The Cowboy and His Horse

Over at the branding chutes, more cowboys work fast and hard. Before the beeves go north they must have a road brand that shows who owns them. Very often a man will buy cattle from several different ranches to make up a herd, and these cattle naturally have different brands. On the trail they all have to be marked alike. One by one, steers from the holding herd go through the chutes. For days the smell of burned hair and wood smoke and sweat hang all around, until the last of the three thousand yellowbacks has had the road brand dabbed on his rump.

Meantime cowboys turn the rest of the cattle back on the range — the bulls with their enormous horns, the cows and newly branded calves, all the steers under four years old, and the mossyhorns — steers too old for beef, but useful as leaders on the range.

The roundup is a tough job from sun-up to dark, but there is a lot of excitement and horseplay around it, too. At last the herd is ready for the trail.

CHAPTER 5

THE TRAIL DRIVE

ONLY THE BEST MEN ARE TAKEN ON THE TRAIL, and there is an even number of them so they can work in pairs. The trail boss figures there should be a man for each 175 cattle. That is as many as one rider can handle. The critters are independent. They have fought off wolves and rustled their own living in winter as well as summer. They can be ornery as sin, and are as fast on their feet as any horse.

Before the long trip north starts, let's take a look at these cowboys who are going along.

The Cowboy and His Horse

They are sitting in saddles, many of which are homemade. On their feet they wear high-heeled boots and spurs. They have broad-brimmed, flat-topped hats. Each man carries a Bowie knife and a heavy Colt pistol. But no one carries a rifle because it makes extra weight for the horse and, hanging in its "boot" on the saddle, it is likely to rub a sore on the horse's side. Not that there aren't rifles along. There are, but they travel in the bed wagon, which goes along with every drive.

Also in the bed wagon each cowboy has a roll containing two blankets, extra clothing, and odds and ends. On the drive the waddies sleep on the ground — no tent, no mattress, no cot.

Important as the bed wagon is, the mess wagon is even more important. It is the headquarters of the trail outfit and the only home the cowboy has for months at a time. The cook, or cookie as he is called, drives the mess wagon which holds all the outfit's food and cooking and eating utensils. On the rear of the wagon is the chuck box which has a door that lets down to become a kind of table.

Early Texas Trail Brands

As the drive begins, everything goes according to plan — and it begins shortly after dawn. First the cowboys "drift" the herd away from the bed ground where they spent the night. Two riders, called point riders, guide a hundred or so steers out ahead. They don't rush matters.

Just as slowly and calmly two swing riders follow along, bringing more cattle with them. Then two flank riders nudge more yellow-backs into the lengthening line. Following behind the last of the cattle are two men riding drag. The uneven, weaving column of longhorns is on its way.

44

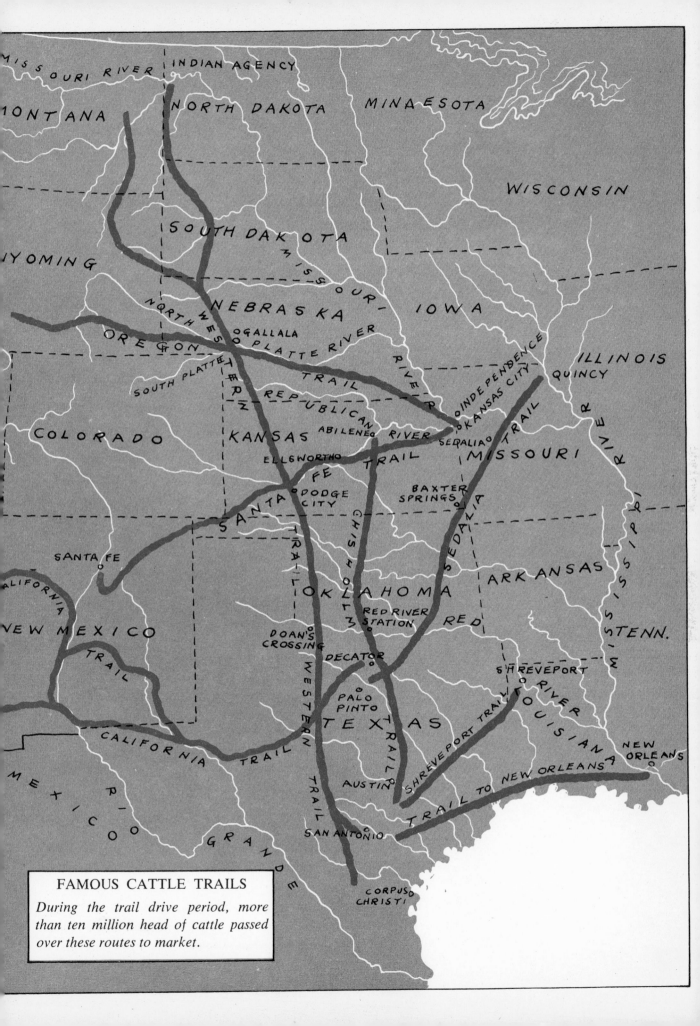

FAMOUS CATTLE TRAILS

During the trail drive period, more than ten million head of cattle passed over these routes to market.

The Cowboy and His Horse

Before long a few old steers, the natural leaders, trot to the head of the line, and they stay there for a thousand miles. The other cattle follow them. Good cowboys soon find out which steers are the leaders. In an hour or so the long line has formed and quieted down. The longhorns have spaced out so their wide horns aren't banging against the horns of their fellows in the column. There is now only a steady cloud of dust, and each cowboy has his big neckerchief pulled up over his nose so he can breathe.

Along to the right of the cattle is the remuda — the extra ponies, upwards of a hundred of them. During a drive cowboys change ponies frequently to give their mounts the rest they need. Already the mess

The most important wagon on the trail drive is the chuck wagon. Here two cowhands start to dismount while the cook, often called "The Perfesser," prepares chow at a table made by letting down the tailgate of the wagon.

46

wagon has creaked and jolted out ahead of the column. There will be a mid-day meal ready when the drive catches up — and again a meal at night.

During the early days of the drive, cowboys push the cattle fairly fast. They know it is easier to handle them once they have left their home range. After that the drive makes only between eight and twelve miles a day. When a herd is trail-broke the cowboys' job is mainly to drift cattle along slowly, letting them graze during the daytime. At night the cowboys take turns riding around the herd to keep it together.

The Trail Drive

The Cowboy and His Horse

On the trail things go much the same day after day. All hands turn out at dawn for breakfast, then throw their bedrolls into the wagon. The wrangler brings in the horses. Each cowboy ropes the horse he wants out of the remuda, saddles it, and goes off to round up the steers who are beginning to wander. Maybe an hour later the herd is back on the Chisholm Trail, headed north.

After the first few nervous days, when the cattle do little feeding, they begin to "eat with the grass," and nobody hurries them. Cowboys just watch out to see that they keep their hot bodies a little distance away from each other in the dust. They know that cattle may suffocate each other if they are too close together — too long.

Ahead of everybody rides the scout who looks for good places for the noon stop and for the bedding down at night. Whenever there

Coyotes, which are small prairie wolves, are regarded by all cattlemen as pests, because even their scent can cause disturbance of cattle bedded down on the trail.

is water, cowboys let longhorns drink all they want to. They know cattle need water at least once a day. This is the way they try to get ahead to drink at a stream. The point, or lead, steers are taken downstream. Then, as more arrive, they go to the stream above the first steers. The last to arrive are the farthest upstream. This way of watering cattle means that each beast has fresh water to drink, at least until others have waded in above it. If the point steers start to drink upstream, they muddy the water for the late-comers below.

RIVER CROSSING

Putting a trail herd across a river can be risky business. Particularly if the river is high in its banks from heavy rains. When a crossing is begun there is no turning back no matter how tough the going gets.

The mess wagon is usually taken over on a small chain ferry, then the remuda put across to show the way. Horses are much better swimmers and far more courageous in the water than cattle. If the longhorns are warm from moving over the trail and the sun is shining the crew drive the point steers into the water in stride. Once they get to swimming for the opposite bank the rest of the herd follows them. But a river crossing is seldom attempted in the late evening when the rays of the setting sun are apt to hit into the steers' eyes and scare them. Cold or rainy weather is another bad time to throw a trail herd across a stream.

You may wonder why cowboys haven't built bridges over the rivers crisscrossing the Chisholm Trail to avoid all this trouble. (There never were but a couple of bridges in all of the thousand miles.) One reason is that cowboys hate to swing an axe, just the way they hate most work they can't do from the saddle. They'll snake into camp a dry mesquite stump at the end of their rope for the cook's fire. But cookie will have to do the chopping. Besides, bridges are easily washed out by flash floods, and they can give way under the pounding hooves of a herd of bawling, jostling longhorns. Then there would be trouble for sure.

The big meal of the day on the long drive is the noon meal. The crew eat in relays. Half eat while half watch the herd. And at this

The Cowboy and His Horse

mid-day stop the hands change to fresh horses. Then the herd is back on the trail again.

As the sun begins to sink in the west, the crew turns the herd off the trail about half a mile and rounds the longhorns up on a suitable

50

bed ground for the night. From eight or nine o'clock until around four in the morning the day herd becomes the night herd. The crew takes turns in two-hour shifts, riding around the bedded-down herd to keep it together. Five hours' sleep a night is the average for a cowboy on a drive, and he gets bone tired and edgy after a hard day in the saddle.

When it comes time to wake a hand so he can take his trick at night riding, you never shake him or even touch him. Startled out of a sound sleep, a cowboy may grab his Colt first and come up shooting. It's safer to wake him by throwing a pebble or twig near him.

Cowboys don't use watches on a drive. They tell time during the day by the position of the sun and at night by watching the movements of the stars. When riding night-herd guard, they manage to keep a pretty close check on the reliefs by following the swing of the Big Dipper.

As they ride they often sing some night-herd song, a slow, easy tune suited in its rhythm to the leisurely pace of their pony. Here is an old-timer that's kept many a bedded-down trail herd quiet:

With their ponies at a slow walk, night herders move around the sleeping cattle in opposite directions. Thus, each rider passes the other twice on a round.

NIGHT-HERDING SONG

Oh, slow up, do-gies, quit mov-ing a - round.

You have wan-dered and tram-pled all o - ver the ground;

Oh, graze a - long, do-gies and feed kind - a slow,

And don't for - ev - er be on the go;

Move slow, lit - tle do - gies, move slow.———

Hi - o, Hi - o,—— Hi - o.———

Oh, slow up, dogies, quit moving around,
You have wandered and trampled all over the ground;
Oh, graze along, dogies, and feed kinda slow,
And don't forever be on the go.
Move slow, little dogies, move slow.
Hi—o, hi—o, hi—o.

Oh, say, little dogies, when you goin' to lay down
And give up this siftin' and roving around?
My horse is leg-weary and I'm awful tired,
But if you get away, I am sure to be fired;
Lay down, little dogies, lay down.
Hi—o, hi—o, hi—o.

Oh, lay still, dogies, since you have laid down,
Stretch away out on the big open ground;
Snore loud, little dogies, and drown the wild sound
That'll go away when the day rolls round,
Lay still, little dogies, lay still.
Hi—o, hi—o, hi—o.

The Cowboy and His Horse

When cowboys riding night herd aren't singing, they call out soothingly to the cattle, turning attention away from any unusual noises which might come out of the dark and frighten them.

About midnight the herd gets restless. All the cattle together lumber to their feet and begin to graze and roam about. Some of the "lone wolves" will try to stray away from the bed ground. Now the cowboys' job is to head up these bunch-quitters and turn them back into the herd. But soon the longhorns have all quieted down again and sleep until daybreak.

Now activity begins once more for both the cattle and the trail crew. The cook has been up since long before dawn, and as the first light appears he sounds his grub call, "Come an' git it afore I drap it in the dirt!"

Another day has started on the old Chisholm Trail.

Many a cowboy has taken a nasty spill and many a cow pony has been badly hurt when the horse has stepped into a badger or prairie dog hole. Sometimes the excitement from a spill has started a stampede.

CHAPTER 6

STAMPEDE!

YOU KNOW NOW THE GENERAL ROUTINE of a cattle drive, but a day's work was seldom as smooth and unruffled as this sounds. Thunderstorms always meant trouble. Too often a lightning bolt would strike and kill a number of cattle, sometimes one of the trail hands. And no man could ever tell when the longhorns might stampede. On stormy, dark nights cowboys kept their night horses picketed near them, saddled and bridled. Some even slept with the reins wrapped around a wrist, to be ready for instant action. For when a herd of Texas yellowbacks "stampeded," all hands had to hit the leather fast. "Tie your hats to the saddle horn, boys! The herd's broke!" was the cattle-trail rally cry.

NIGHT STAMPEDE ON

Here is what one trail boss wrote in his diary, about an actual stampede on the Chisholm that involved a number of cattle drives:

"*June 1*. Stampede last night among 6 droves — a general mix-up and loss of beeves. Hunt cattle again. Men all tired and want to leave. Spent the day separating Beeves and Hunting. Two men and a Bunch of Beeves lost. Many men in trouble. Horses all give out and men refused to do anything.

56

THE CHISHOLM TRAIL

"*June 2*. Hard rain and wind storm. Beeves ran and had to be on Horseback all night. Awful night. Wet all night. Clear bright morning. Men still lost. Quit the Beeves to go Hunting men is the word. 4 P.M. Found our men with Indian and 195 Beeves 14 miles from camp. All most starved not having a bite to eat for 60 hours. Got all to the camp about 12 P.M. Tired."

One big danger was a pony throwing a foot in a badger hole and spilling the rider out of the saddle in the path of the onrushing cattle. When that happened the cowboy usually had to be buried where he was found because he wasn't in any shape to be carried back to the wagon.

Almost any sudden or unexpected noise might scare a trail herd at night and change it into a fright-crazed mass which thundered off in any direction at terrific speed. A horse shaking itself after long hours under the saddle, the scent of a coyote, even the faint rustle of a jack rabbit running by could touch off the fireworks. If a run wasn't stopped short the cows sometimes scattered for twenty or thirty or up to forty miles. And that meant plenty of hard riding hunting them down.

It was a real job to break up a stampede and bring the herd under control. The riders first had to get ahead of the cattle in the dark, make the leaders swerve and change direction, throwing them back on the trail, until finally the cows had slowed down and were milling in a circle.

TRAIL THIEVES

Accidental stampedes could be very bad business, and so could stampedes that gangs of trail thieves started on purpose. These hard-bitten renegades would get a herd running at night and then hole up several hundred critters in some hide-out gully where they held them until the trail boss "bought" them back. Sometimes, after starting a run like this, they would offer to help the crew find the "lost" cattle at, say, a dollar a head. Of course, they only helped in the hunt if they got paid.

Once in a while one of these gangs of desperadoes — they were called jayhawkers in Kansas — just plain murdered a trail crew and made off with the whole herd. No wonder cowboys were particular about the way they were awakened at night.

Cattle thieves had dozens of tricks. They were the pirates of the cow country and the cattle trails, and later on in this book you'll read more about them because there is almost as much rustling going on now as in the old days.

As the great trail herds followed the Pole Star northward they often reached the cow towns at the railroads with several more head of cattle than they started with. These extra animals were strays that had drifted into the trail herd from the ranges through which the drive passed. To stop this kind of thing local cowmen got laws passed giving them the right to appoint "rep" men (rep is short for representative). The reps inspected the trail herds and cut out the critters they found carrying local brands. But reps didn't stop these losses entirely. Smart rustlers sometimes posed as reps and showed fake credentials. With these they got away with lots of cattle.

In Indian Territory, the trail herds usually had to hand over some longhorns to the Indians, who considered they were entitled to the cattle as payment for the right to trail the drives over their land.

A band of some thirty Osage or "Shave Heads" headed west for the buffalo country might meet a drive. Having their women and children along, they weren't hostile any, but insisted the trail boss pay a toll of three or four steers. The trail boss agreed and had several "cripples" — the poorest animals in the herd — cut out of the drag. Whooping and yelling, the young bucks would chase the steers wildly across the prairie and shoot them down. In fifteen minutes the carcasses would be butchered and loaded on the travois and the band would be on its way again.

CHAPTER 7

COWBOYS IN CALIFORNIA

THE BIG CATTLE DRIVES, which began with the coming of railroads, stopped with the coming of fences. Barbed wire ended the Trail Drive Era as suddenly as railroads started it.

By 1880 ranchers had fenced in much of the best grazing land in the West. Where water was scarce, they wanted all of it for their own cattle. It became impossible to have drives in the old way and, besides, the railroads kept getting closer and closer to the big ranches. So naturally it was no longer necessary to raise cattle which could last out the drives. Longhorns, which had wonderful endurance, disappeared from the ranches. Brahma cattle imported from Asia were much bigger and made better beef steers. Brought into south Texas, they replaced the longhorns there, and heavy Hereford cattle became favorites in other parts of the West.

As hundreds and hundreds of fenced-in cattle spreads took the place of the open range, the lives of cowboys changed. Cattle became more valuable and were given more care.

On the open range there had always been some cowboys who were line riders. This meant that they rode around the part of the range where one rancher had his cattle. Line riders kept other cattle from straying onto the range. But now fences did that job, if the fences were in good repair. So the cowboys' work now included fence riding. They checked every bit of fence once or twice a week to make sure the wire was up and the posts in good condition.

THE VAQUEROS OF OLD CALIFORNIA

Life for the cowboy settled down to be a lot like it is today. But before we take a good look at the modern cowboy, let's make a quick trip to California where cowmen had a different history from those in Texas. The first California vaqueros were descendants of the Spanish in Mexico, just as the Texans were. But they brought cows and horses to California in 1769 — long before there were any cattle, at least, in Texas. It wasn't long, though, until the missions and the rich landowners needed a lot more vaqueros than had come up from Mexico. So they trained the Indians to handle horses and cattle. The Indians of course had never seen either a horse or a cow before, but many soon learned the tricks of riding and roping.

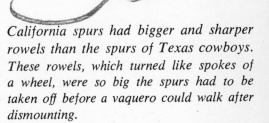

California spurs had bigger and sharper rowels than the spurs of Texas cowboys. These rowels, which turned like spokes of a wheel, were so big the spurs had to be taken off before a vaquero could walk after dismounting.

61

The Cowboy and His Horse

For the most part these Indian vaqueros did things about the same way vaqueros in Mexico did, but as time went on they made changes in their clothes and in their tools. They liked to wear huge rowels on their spurs, for instance. The rowels were so big that a vaquero had to take them off in order to walk. A poor vaquero had to take off his own spurs, but a rich caballero always had an Indian peon do this for him.

In the early days in California, missions owned many of the largest cattle ranches. Here we see the Mission of Santa Barbara, where Indians were trained as cowhands. Ox-drawn carts like the one in the foreground were used to carry hides and tallow to the seaports.

As the California vaquero did more and more riding and roping, he changed his saddle. The cinch on the old Spanish saddle was attached to the very front near the horn. But the vaquero found that his saddle stayed on better when he was dallying if the cinch was attached at the center.

There were times when a vaquero wanted to be plenty sure his saddle stayed where he had cinched it. For instance, a group of daring young fellows would get it into their heads to go on a grizzly bear hunt. The idea was to bring the bear back alive. So the knives they carried strapped to their legs weren't much use, and peons weren't allowed to have guns anyway. Their braided rawhide reatas were the tools to use.

A grizzly could slip out of one of those ropes more easily than a horse or cow. He would bite one in two. He could, and sometimes did, turn and charge the man who had dropped a noose over his head,

or on one of his feet. Roping grizzlies was about the riskiest sport
cowboys ever invented, but California vaqueros could do it. Then
they would trick the bear into walking back to the rancho himself.
They couldn't lead a big grizzly, or even drag him. So they teased
him into lunging after them, chasing them back to a strong pen which
was ready to hold even the angriest animal. Later the vaqueros would
tie the grizzly and a bull together and watch them fight.

64

The spoor of the grizzly bear.

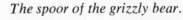

While the early Mexican vaqueros used to hunt grizzlies for sport, today's cowboy knows that there are few more dangerous menaces on the range than a she-bear protecting her cubs. Though modern cowhands on Northwestern ranches seldom seek out such encounters, they are quick on the draw and ready to handle the situation.

This dangerous game was only one of the ways vaqueros showed their daring and skill. They also liked to bury a live rooster in the ground, all except its head. Then they would gallop past at top speed, lean way over in the saddle and try to grab the rooster's head. Of course when a vaquero caught the head he broke the bird's neck, but he also risked his own neck. It was not easy to hang way down to the ground on one side of a galloping cow pony.

The Cowboy and His Horse

The vaqueros' work was not easy to do either, but most of it was like the work in Texas. Californians and Texans in the early days rounded up cattle mainly for their hides and tallow. Sailing ships from Boston would stop all along the California coastline in search of hides and tallow. When the ships came, their holds were filled with all kinds of things the remote Californians were glad to have a chance to buy. There were fancy clothing and furniture for the rich caballeros, and for the poor vaqueros there were simpler things, if they were lucky enough to have any money. But rich and poor alike bought all they could. These Boston ships were almost the only contact with the great outer world.

When the ship captains sold their goods to a rancher they usually got his promise to pay a month or two later in hides and tallow. Then big roundups began. While the ships moved on to other points along the coast, vaqueros scoured the ranges for cattle, and horses too. Indian peons skinned the animals, tanned the hides, and melted tallow out of the fat. They made big bags out of some of the hides and stored the tallow in them. A couple of months later the ship came back and picked up its payment.

A few times there were big roundups even when no ships were waiting to pick up cargo. Some of these roundups, or rodeos, came during droughts when there wasn't nearly enough grass to feed all the cattle and horses. Vaqueros then would use their sharp-pointed pikes to spear hundreds and thousands of the animals as they galloped along beside them. Or they would even drive whole bands of wild horses or herds of cattle over a cliff into the sea. This may sound cruel but it was the only way to save the lives of those that were left.

All this kind of thing happened long before the days of the big cattle hunts in Texas. There were cowboys in California more than

An early California saddle with a removable "mochilla" behind the cantle for an extra rider. Note also the large, semi-circular tapaderos, the leather coverings over the stirrups to protect cowboys' boots from thorns and rough brush.

fifty years before Mexican settlers began to move into Texas. But cattle raising in California changed rapidly after 1848.

From the beginning in California, Catholic missions had owned big ranches. One mission alone had something like a hundred thousand cattle and horses. When California became part of the United States, the Mexican soldiers there lost their power, and the missions did, too. All the big ranches found it harder to get Indians to work for them. And the gold rush, which began almost at the same time, brought thousands of new people to California from the United States — and everywhere else.

Cowboys in California

One of these settlers was a German named Henry Miller. He stepped off a ship in San Francisco one day with only a few dollars in his pocket — and not many years later he owned most of the ranches and cattle in California. Miller began by buying two cows from a couple of vaqueros who wanted cash for a good time in the big city. Then Miller butchered the cattle right on the street and sold the beef to passers-by. In one day he had much more money than he had landed with. The growing population of San Francisco wanted more and more meat, so Miller got vaqueros and big ranch owners to sell him cattle. And he always lent them money when they were broke — which was most of the time. Then he would let them pay off their debts by giving him cattle or land in exchange. He sold his cattle but he never sold the land. Soon, most of the cowmen in the state were working for him.

Another type of early California saddle, this one featuring circular tapaderos and bearskin saddle bags.

Miller was very careful to try to keep on friendly terms with all these former ranchers and their former vaqueros. He was a stranger who, in some way most people couldn't quite savvy, suddenly owned everything all by himself. One way Miller kept friends was to observe the old custom that any man who needed food could kill a beef as long as he left the hide where it would show on a fence. Miller could

The Cowboy and His Horse

even make friends among robbers. He was held up on a remote road one time, and the robbers took everything he had. But Miller knew some change always came in handy, so he asked the robbers if they would lend him two dollars out of what they had stolen. They agreed and then rode happily off to spend their new wealth. Some time later Miller saw these same two highwaymen in town and, instead of trying to get them punished, he paid them back the two dollars he had borrowed!

With the coming of Henry Miller, the old happy-go-lucky days of the feudal Spanish landowners disappeared. Instead Henry Miller turned cattle raising into a business, and he paid wages to the vaqueros, who in the old Spanish days had been peons working only for food and shelter. Miller found a growing market for beef in the expanding population, and of course he kept on making money from hides.

As the entire cattle business in California grew, cowboys came there from Texas, and from all over the West. They also learned some of the Californians' ways and took them back across the Rocky Mountains as they continued their wandering. Most cowboys east of California traveled around a great deal over the vast cow country. They were usually footloose bachelors, and a lot of the time they had to move on from one ranch to another looking for work. But the Californians were different. They had never had to do much traveling in search of work. They just became cowboys on the ranches where they had been born, and they stayed near by all their lives. Also they were often married and had children. That is one more difference between Californios, as they were called, and other cowboys in the past. Nowadays many cowboys everywhere have families and wander a lot less than they used to, but you'll read about that later. First, let's follow the cowboys of today as they do their work around the year.

68

Good cowboys always rope a calf by "heeling" it — that is, throwing the noose so that it snares the hind legs.

CHAPTER 8

SPRING ROUNDUP

IN THE SPRING cowboys have always rounded up cattle in order to brand new calves. There was branding along with the roundup of longhorns for market during the Trail Drive Era. And there is a spring roundup for calf branding today.

In the Southwest, cowboys begin to get ready for the roundup in early April. On the northern ranges they start about the first of May. But the work is pretty much the same on any big spread, and there

The Cowboy and His Horse

is plenty of it. The ranch foreman hires extra hands until he has a crew of nine cowboys. They repair corrals and see that all the horses are shod.

The cook repairs the chuck wagon, which is much like the wagon used on big cattle drives long ago. Then he fills it with supplies. He puts in water barrels, groceries, eating and table utensils, Dutch ovens, fire-stakes and bar, firewood for emergencies, spare equipment and the crew's bedrolls. The flat-bed wagon has compartments for these things, so the cook can fasten them tight and keep them from joggling all around in rough country.

A cowboy's bedroll usually has a couple of blankets or comforters — soogans — wrapped up in a big canvas tarpaulin called a tarp. This roll is a suitcase as well as a bed, for it holds spare clothes and a war bag which may have almost anything in it — an extra shirt and socks, a sewing kit, toilet articles, precious letters and souvenirs, even a horseshoe, not so much for good luck as because its owner may need it for his horse.

In the spring steers often wander into water holes and get bogged down. When a cowboy ropes a steer and pulls him onto dry ground with the rope tied to his saddle horn, he says he is "bog riding." And he knows he had better get out of the steer's way in a hurry. Steers who have been dragged are never grateful and usually charge their rescuer.

70

During the roundup, a cowboy sleeps on the ground. He calls it his Tucson bed. There isn't room to take cots in the chuck wagon and, besides, it's warmer on the ground. With part of the tarp under him to keep out dampness, and part over him as protection against rain, he has a sleeping bag. But a cowboy doesn't brag about his comfort. He says he "lays on his stomach and covers himself with his back."

Before dawn on the day the roundup begins, the roundup boss shouts, "Roll up and roll out." That's the signal to tie up the bedrolls and put them on the wagon. Then after breakfast the wagon, followed by the wrangler and the remuda and the cowboys, heads out for the range. By night, the first camp has been made, maybe at the edge of a creek, and next day the hard work begins.

Some of the men ride circle. Here is what happens. The riders get going from camp shortly after daybreak. Their job is to comb every part of a definite section of the range and gather up all the cattle there. Three or four miles from camp, the circle riders begin to drop out at half-mile intervals. In this fashion they divide up the territory

and head back toward camp, each one driving all the cattle he can — usually about fifty or sixty head at a time.

As these bunches arrive, a couple of cowboys keep them in a loose herd and let them rest. While the loose herding goes on, circle riders keep bringing in more cattle, until they have scoured the whole area in a big circle around the camp. Often they travel fifty to seventy-five miles in a day. Of course, they have to change mounts frequently, and a circle rider may have fifteen horses to choose from. He calls them his string. He gets a fresh horse from his string back at camp whenever he needs one.

It generally takes three or four days to round up all the cattle near one camp. Sometimes a cowboy can wear himself out pushing through heavy brush for hours after just one cow and her calf, but it's his job to bring in every single critter.

When the gather is finished, some of the cowboys drive the whole herd to branding corrals. Meanwhile the cook loads his wagon and moves to a new camp where circle riders begin all over again. The others will catch up with the wagon before too long. They can do the branding very quickly once they get started.

The Cowboy and His Horse

72

CHAPTER 9

BRANDS
AND BRANDING

IN THE BRANDING CORRAL, the cutter, who rides a specially trained cutting pony, turns quietly into the herd, picks out a cow and calf, and works them to the edge of the gather. Then he heels the calf —that is, he ropes it by the hind legs. With his lariat dallied around his saddle horn, he drags the calf to the branding fire and turns it over to a couple of cowboys called flankers. One flanker reaches across the calf's back with both arms and grabs the animal either

The Cowboy and His Horse

under the throat or under a hind leg. With a quick jerk, he lifts the calf, swings it off the ground, and drops it on its right side or flank. Holding his right knee on the calf's neck, he grabs the left forefoot, bends it back and pulls it as high as he can in the air. The other flanker gets hold of the left rear leg, pulls it up high, and stands with both feet on the right rear leg. The critter is helpless, and the third member of the branding team, the iron man, can go to work. He keeps a supply of branding irons cherry red, as he says, over a fire. He takes one and presses it quickly against the calf's left hip. Then the fourth member of the team cuts the owner's earmark on the calf's left ear and, if it is a male, castrates it. All this takes less than half a minute, but the calf is bawling plenty and makes a dash for its mother the second it is let up.

During the roundup, some late calves are born, and they are branded, too. The old dry cows are cut out of the herd for shipment to market. The others are turned back on the range. Sometimes on Texas ranches the year-old calves, or yearlings, are separated from their mothers and sent to ranches farther north where they are fattened for market.

Early Southwest brands, many over 100 years old.

By June, most of the work has been done. Now the extra hands are laid off. They go to town and spend their money, or they ride from ranch to ranch looking for work. Wherever they go, they know they will be welcome if they don't loaf around too long eating free meals. While cowboys are looking for work, they say they are riding the chuck line.

The regular ranch hands stay on all year round. One of their chores, summer and winter, is to ride fence. And they repair any breaks they find, so that cattle won't wander. Sometimes fences don't just break down accidentally. Rustlers cut the wire, and they have a lot of tricky ways of making off with the cattle. Which brings us back to branding — the real point of the spring roundup.

74

A brand is a kind of private trade mark or signature which the owner has burned on a calf's hide, and it stays as long as the critter lives. It is the best — and oldest — way of telling who owns an animal.

Brands and Branding

In the early days of the open range, there were no fences to keep one man's cattle separate from another's, but cowboys needed a way of telling which was which. Brands were the best way. When the ranchers settled down after the Civil War, everybody agreed that a calf should bear the same brand as its mother. So, at one roundup there would be many different branding irons, and a rep from each ranch in the area would see that everything was done fair and square.

CATTLE RUSTLERS

From the very beginning rustlers had a way of sneaking onto ranges and dabbing their own brand on unbranded calves. Then they claimed them at the roundup. They also roped branded cattle and blotted the brands—that is, they changed a brand to look like a totally different one. At the roundup they got away with these cattle unless someone could prove that brands were being blotted. Rustlers also used slow brands — that is, brands which are not officially registered. When they do this, they always want to get away with the cattle quickly before they are discovered.

In the early days, there weren't any law courts in cow country. When a thief was caught, the cattlemen themselves acted as judge and jury, and the punishment for stealing was hanging — a necktie party.

Nowadays the cattlemen have associations that hire special guards and detectives — in Texas they are called Texas Rangers — who catch rustlers and take them to regular law courts. Death is no longer the penalty for cattle stealing, but many a rancher, whose cows turned up with too many calves, is sitting in prison right now, wishing he hadn't been so handy with a running iron.

Brands are useful to ranchers as advertisements, too. Cattle buyers know the brands of the ranches with the best grade of cattle, and they pay more for them.

The Cowboy and His Horse

There are many reasons why cattlemen want their stock branded. And there are complicated laws and regulations so that everyone can tell which brand is whose. Brands in Texas and everywhere else are registered in books which anybody can buy. You can see why this is necessary if you know that in Texas alone there have been at least half a million brands listed at one time or another.

HOW BRANDS BEGAN

Maybe you would like to know more about how this system of branding got started and some of the changes that have taken place over the years, because to lots of people branding is one of the most interesting of cattle country practices. So far as anyone knows, branding started way back in Egypt. Pictures have been found on tombs in Thebes dating back to more than two thousand years before the birth of Christ.

They say that the followers of Cortez were the first to use brands in North America, shortly after their invasion of Mexico. You saw the brand, composed of three crosses, back on page 15. And, just as the vaquero of Old Mexico was himself the forerunner of our American cowboy, so the practice of cattle branding came north from Mexico.

These early Spanish-Mexican brands were very ornate and, from

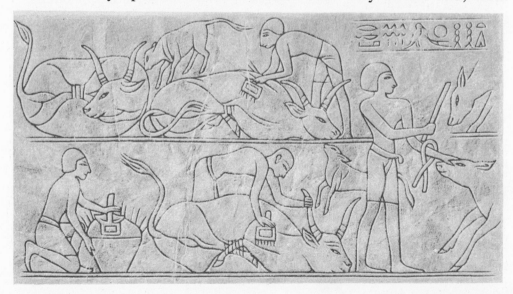

Reconstructed drawing of branding in Ancient Egypt, circa 1500 B.C.

76

an artistic standpoint, very beautiful. Several handsome examples of these early brands are shown here.

But by the time the early Texas cattle raiser began gathering large herds, he began to simplify his brand because there were just too many cattle and too little time to bother with fancy scrollwork. In those days every cowboy riding range carried a "running iron" as part of his saddle gear and whenever he'd run across a maverick or unbranded dogie, he'd simply hogtie the critter and run the boss' brand on its hide right then and there.

Brands and Branding

So the brands themselves became simplified and instead of the fancy Mexican-style brands, simple squares, circles and triangles in combination with a letter or letters from the owner's name came into use.

In some cases the owners made puns on their names or used simple pictures to illustrate their names. H. A. Tutt's brand and the brand of W. G. Mulkey are good examples of this practice. And one of the funniest of these joking brands is that of Mrs. W. G. Potts of Dickens County, Texas.

H. A. Tutt Brand

RUNNING AND STAMP IRONS

For quite a few years these "running" brands were in general use but, as the cattle industry became more prosperous and more rustlers were moving in on established herds, owners found that it was much easier for these more-or-less slap-dash brands to be altered into the rustler's "slow brand" you have already read about. So most ranchers adopted the stamp iron technique—using irons with the complete design already stamped on it. Generally speaking they changed to smaller size brands, too, because the value of the steer's hide was increasing and they didn't want it all scarred up with brand marks.

Mulkey Brand

Potts Brand

To fool rustlers, though, many ranchers started putting brands in two or three different places—hip, shoulder and side—instead of just one place.

There were several other reasons for branding in more than one place, though. First off, it made things a lot easier for the range rider in early spring roundup because at that time many cattle have not yet shed their winter coats of hair and the chances are that at least one brand mark will still be hidden. Also lots of ranchers found that, in the haste of branding a large herd during roundup, some calves were branded so lightly that the branded area would peel off in a year or so.

As a matter of fact there grew up so much suspicion of "running" brands that some sections of the country outlawed them and any waddy found on the open range with a running iron was considered almost certain to be a rustler. Even so, some small spreads—even today—use the running iron for branding, though almost all big outfits use the stamp iron.

Modern Stamp Irons.

VENT BRANDS

Every time a steer is sold, the brand of the old owner has to be crossed out and the new owner's brand burned in. Since this is done at the time of the sale, the brand used is called the vent brand, from the Spanish word *venta*, "sale." It usually is a crossed bar but sometimes may be a blank or "blind" iron. Occasionally a steer changes ownership many times during its life and, of course, the old brand must be vented and the new one inserted each time. In such a case the steer is said to be "burnt till it looks like a brand book."

THE "MURDER" STEER

Back in the colorful days when the West was young, disputes about brands were frequent—and sometimes the arguments led to gunplay. One of the most famous incidents occurred down in the Big Bend country of Texas. Two ranch hands from rival spreads, Gilleland and Poe by name, got into a heated argument about whose brand was to be run on a yearling in a pool roundup.

Finally Gilleland drew his gun and killed Poe. As the story goes, he never gave Poe a chance to draw his gun and that—under frontier law—made Gilleland guilty of deliberate murder.

Some of the quick-tempered onlookers started throwing lead themselves and when the smoke had cleared, four hands from the rival spreads had been killed and the guilty party, Gilleland, had hit the leather for parts unknown.

Feelings were running mighty high, as a result, so some of the other waddies roped the yearling that had started all the argument and in foot-high letters across its side branded the word MURDER.

According to legend, the steer became an outcast, wandering from

79

spread to spread year after year. Shunned by all as a symbol of foul and unavenged crime, its story has lived on and even now the tale of the "Murder" steer is often retold around western campfires.

"HOT AS HELL" HITSON

One of the most dramatic tales of brands and branding comes from New Mexico. As two range riders were making their rounds in the Spring of 1871 they came upon a longhorn straggler with a strange brand marking all over one side of the critter. When they fetched up with the steer they could read this cryptic brand:

7-4-68 INDIANS HOT AS HELL JH

Naturally they brought the steer back to the corral and, after checking around, were able to piece together the story behind this most unusual brand. It seems that three years before (1868) a young cowhand, name of Jess Hitson, went off to range-brand some strays on the Colorado spread he was working for. He had never been seen or heard of after that day—and the brand on the steer they had found in New Mexico told why.

Attacked by Indians, probably Apaches, just after roping a dogie, Hitson realized that the only chance he had of getting his story to his friends was to brand it into the hide of the dogie. So, while the Indians circled in on him, he hastily wrote his gallant—and humorous—message. "Hot as hell" he wrote, and doubtless he referred to his own predicament as well as to the weather. Thus, in writing his own obituary, Jess Hitson added another brave chapter to the picturesque history of the American cowboy.

Probably no system of communication or identification ever created by man has become quite so complex in quite so short a time as has the language of American cattle brands. In little more than a century and a half a unique and, to the untrained eye, completely baffling series of signs and symbols has been devised and one of the more bewildering aspects of brands is that the same brand can be read differently in different parts of the country. For instance, a certain brand means C Bar C in one brand district of Arizona and Capital X in another.

But there are a few basic rules that all brand creators seem to follow and, with their help, you may be able to work out for yourself the names of the brands of the following pages.

As a rule, brands are called from left to right as you look at them, and from the top down and the outside in. A short horizontal line ▬ if placed above or below, or to the right or left of another mark, is called a *Bar*. When used in a vertical position **|** , it becomes a *One;* if extended ▬▬ it is called a *Line* or *Rail*. When a *One* is slanted to the right or left \\/ it is a *Slash*. The letter A minus its center bar ∧ is read as an *Open A*. The same mark, if run above another symbol becomes a *Rafter,* sometimes called a *Half-Diamond*. Thus the ⩓7 brand is read as the Rafter 7.

Next is the *Box* or *Square* ▢ and the *Half-Box* ⊓, which may also be called a *Staple*. An elongated *Box* ▭ is known as a *Block*. Other basic forms are the *Diamond* ◇ , the *Triangle* △, the *Circle* ◯, the *Half-Circle* ∩ , and the *Quarter-Circle* ⌒. The last named mark, if placed under and touching another symbol, becomes a *Rocker,* and the brand � is read as the Rocking H. In like manner, the *Bracket* ⌐ when used beneath and touching another mark becomes a *Bench*. For example, the brand ⸂Y⸃ is called the Bracket Y, while the ⊥ mark is read Y On A Bench, or more probably Y At A Meeting, by the cowboy. Finally a small circle ◯ is known as a *Hole,* while a still smaller solid circle ● is a *Dot* or *Period*.

Brands and Branding

*The Cowboy
and
His Horse*

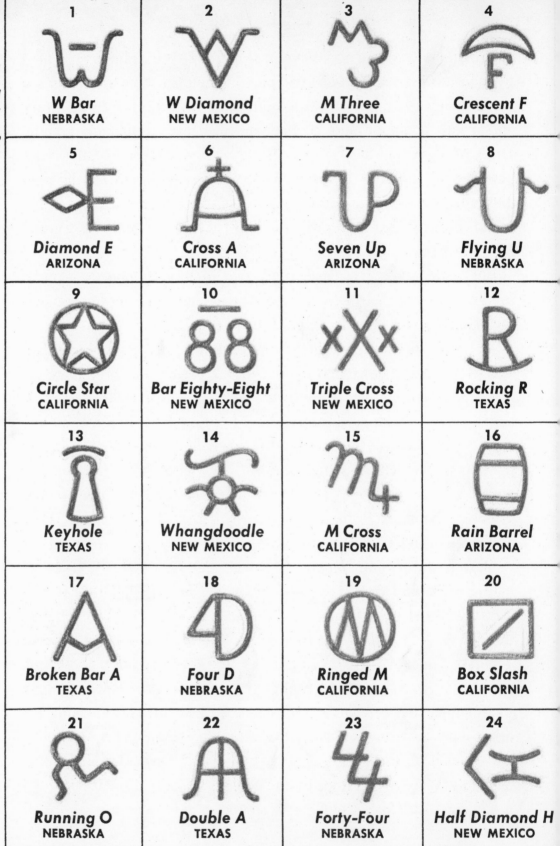

1	2	3	4
W Bar NEBRASKA	**W Diamond** NEW MEXICO	**M Three** CALIFORNIA	**Crescent F** CALIFORNIA
5	6	7	8
Diamond E ARIZONA	**Cross A** CALIFORNIA	**Seven Up** ARIZONA	**Flying U** NEBRASKA
9	10	11	12
Circle Star CALIFORNIA	**Bar Eighty-Eight** NEW MEXICO	**Triple Cross** NEW MEXICO	**Rocking R** TEXAS
13	14	15	16
Keyhole TEXAS	**Whangdoodle** NEW MEXICO	**M Cross** CALIFORNIA	**Rain Barrel** ARIZONA
17	18	19	20
Broken Bar A TEXAS	**Four D** NEBRASKA	**Ringed M** CALIFORNIA	**Box Slash** CALIFORNIA
21	22	23	24
Running O NEBRASKA	**Double A** TEXAS	**Forty-Four** NEBRASKA	**Half Diamond H** NEW MEXICO

25 **Triangle B** TEXAS	**26** **Safety Pin** NEW MEXICO	**27** **Heart Four Bar** TEXAS	**28** **Keno** TEXAS
29 **Rafter Diamond** TEXAS	**30** **O K** TEXAS	**31** **Bow And Arrow** NEW MEXICO	**32** **Bracket Compass** MONTANA
33 **Saddle Horn** NEW MEXICO	**34** **Circle A Bar** CALIFORNIA	**35** **Rafter J** NEW MEXICO	**36** **Triangle Circle** CALIFORNIA
37 **Broken Heart** NEW MEXICO	**38** **Music** NEBRASKA	**39** **Bar Forty** TEXAS	**40** **Quarter Circle W** NEW MEXICO
41 **Boot Jack** TEXAS	**42** **Crescent E** NEBRASKA	**43** **Flag Bar** CALIFORNIA	**44** **Two Bit** ARIZONA
45 **Hanging O** TEXAS	**46** **Three Dot W** CALIFORNIA	**47** **Dinner Bell** CALIFORNIA	**48** **Barbeque** TEXAS

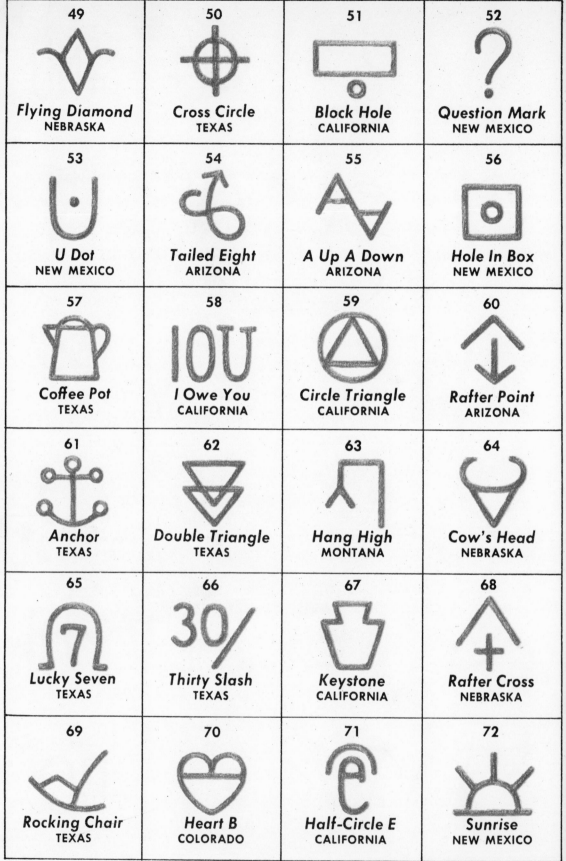

49 Flying Diamond NEBRASKA	50 Cross Circle TEXAS	51 Block Hole CALIFORNIA	52 Question Mark NEW MEXICO
53 U Dot NEW MEXICO	54 Tailed Eight ARIZONA	55 A Up A Down ARIZONA	56 Hole In Box NEW MEXICO
57 Coffee Pot TEXAS	58 I Owe You CALIFORNIA	59 Circle Triangle CALIFORNIA	60 Rafter Point ARIZONA
61 Anchor TEXAS	62 Double Triangle TEXAS	63 Hang High MONTANA	64 Cow's Head NEBRASKA
65 Lucky Seven TEXAS	66 Thirty Slash TEXAS	67 Keystone CALIFORNIA	68 Rafter Cross NEBRASKA
69 Rocking Chair TEXAS	70 Heart B COLORADO	71 Half-Circle E CALIFORNIA	72 Sunrise NEW MEXICO

73	74	75	76
Diamond N ARIZONA	**Fish Hook** ARIZONA	**Two Bar X** TEXAS	**Pig Pen** TEXAS

77	78	79	80
Rafter Hole Bar NEBRASKA	**Covered Star** NEBRASKA	**Arrow J** CALIFORNIA	**Box W** TEXAS

81	82	83	84
Specs CALIFORNIA	**Bridle Bit** TEXAS	**Circle Dot** NEW MEXICO	**Hash Knife** TEXAS

85	86	87	88
Tumbling A TEXAS	**Leaning H Bar** NEBRASKA	**Scissors** NEW MEXICO	**T In Block** TEXAS

89	90	91	92
Diamond Lazy S NEW MEXICO	**Lined M** NEBRASKA	**Circle Two Bar** NEBRASKA	**Wind Vane** TEXAS

93	94	95	96
Arrow E CALIFORNIA	**Triangle Slash** NEBRASKA	**Swing Easy** WYOMING	**Three O'Clock** CALIFORNIA

The Cowboy and His Horse

While branding is the most common method of identifying beef cattle, almost all large ranchers also "earmark" their herds. An earmark is exactly what the word implies — a mark on the ear made by cutting. It may be made on either or both ears. There are several common types of earmarks—crop, overslope, underslope, swallow fork, steeple fork and others—which are shown on this page.

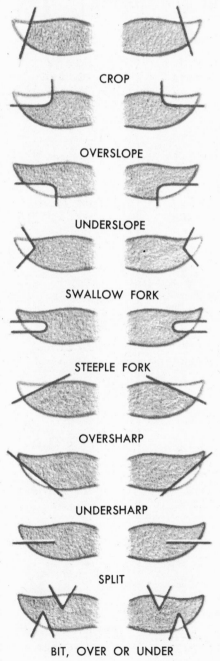

CROP

OVERSLOPE

UNDERSLOPE

SWALLOW FORK

STEEPLE FORK

OVERSHARP

UNDERSHARP

SPLIT

BIT, OVER OR UNDER

Now there are many reasons why ranchers want to earmark their cattle, in addition to branding them. But the two most important reasons are that it makes it easy to identify a cow head-on — because cattle usually put their ears forward when being approached from the front — and also the earmark furnishes a positive identification even during seasons of the year when the cow's heavy winter coat may make the burned brand unreadable. These marks are recorded in the official registry books along with the burned brand.

On most large spreads, this ear-marking is done at the same time the calves are branded and dehorned and the whole operation usually takes only a few minutes, if an experienced team of cowhands is handling the job.

86

CHAPTER 10

BIG SPREADS IN TEXAS

IN TEXAS WHERE THE GREAT CATTLE DRIVES BEGAN, there are still some of the biggest ranches in the world. The long-horns have gone, except for a few that are kept as curiosities here and there. Bigger, beefier cattle have taken their place. Some are descended from hump-backed Brahma that were imported from India and crossed with longhorns to produce an animal that is heavy but can live well on the range. Many of the cattle on Texas ranges now are the white-faced Herefords, which came from England.

The Cowboy and His Horse

The King Ranch—called the world's biggest—has produced a new type of cattle, the Santa Gertrudis, which is part Brahma and part shorthorn. This huge spread is really four separate ranches, covering 1,250,000 acres. That is as much territory altogether as half the State of Delaware. In fact, the King Ranch has its own representative in Congress.

The old-time ways of the Mexican vaqueros are still followed there, and the ranch hands themselves are Mexicans. Mounted on special sorrel horses bred on the ranch, the vaqueros ride herd on 125,000 cattle. But they combine their traditional skills with new-fangled ways of doing things. Instead of driving herds to distant watering holes, they just head the animals toward one of the 250 windmills that pump water from wells.

MODERN METHODS ON WORLD'S LARGEST RANCH

For building or repairing the 1500 miles of fences, they use electric drills instead of hammers and staples. Here and there on the range are the ranch's own filling stations so that cars or pick-up trucks won't run out of gas in covering the vast territory.

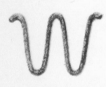

Running W Brand
KING RANCH

Even the ancient Spanish pike has been modernized on the King ranch. It's still used to prod cattle, not along roads but into railroad stock cars. And it's now equipped with electricity, so a mild shock nudges slow-moving steers along.

On one part or another of the ranch, grass is always ready for grazing, and there are cattle drives at different times of the year to shift the critters from one pasture to another. Concrete bunk houses dot the distant parts of the spread, so that range-riding vaqueros seldom have to sleep out in the open any more.

J A Brand

Tents shelter the cowpokes and their bedrolls on the JA Ranch—another big Texas spread up in the northwest part of the state. Out on the great flat prairie they get shade at mealtime from a canvas fly stretched out behind the chuck wagon. About the only other shade a man gets is when he's on the ground in the shadow of his horse.

Here cowboy life is much as it has always been. At roundup time the cook bakes biscuits in the dutch ovens while the hoodlum chops wood. (He's the one who drives the bed wagon.)

Another thing about cow country that hasn't changed is the rustler problem. But some Texas ranchers have a new way of riding rustler patrol. They scout around in airplanes, and at the same time they can see whether the cattle should be shifted to better grazing land. At roundup time, too, a man in a plane can locate cattle hiding in the brush more quickly than a man on horseback.

In these new developments in ranching, Texas leads the whole country just as Texas cowboys have always set the style in everything throughout most of the spreads of the West. For a hundred years Texas has been looked at as the real home of most cowpokes—and it still is.

Big Spread in Texas

CHAPTER 11

THE COWBOY'S EQUIPMENT

BY LOOKING BACK at the pictures of old-time cowboys you can get a pretty good idea of the way they dress today. Things haven't changed much. A cowboy has clothes and tools to fit his needs while he is at work branding and roping and riding circle. There's a reason for everything he wears and for the gear he uses.

Take his hat, for instance: living outdoors, exposed to all kinds of weather, he found long ago that cheap wool hats wouldn't stand the wear and tear. So, when the John B. Stetson Company of Philadelphia put out a good grade of felt hat, cowboys promptly tried it, decided it was what they needed, and have stayed with a "John B." ever since. This "ten-gallon" hat serves as a sunshade on hot days and an umbrella when it rains. The brim can be tied down with a neckerchief for ear muffs, and ear muffs come in mighty handy on the cold northern ranges.

Roping broncs, branding calves, riding herd and rounding up cattle are usually hot and dusty jobs. Sweat runs into a cow waddie's eyes, almost blinding him. He wants a handkerchief to wipe his face and eyes with, and he doesn't want to poke around in his pockets looking for one and then have to put it back again. So he simply knots his handkerchief at the back of his neck, and lets it hang down loosely in front, where he can grab it quickly when he needs it. When he lets it go, it is there to flutter and dry in the wind. This same handkerchief, which is usually white, tan or yellow, serves as a muffler in chilly weather. A cowboy can also use it to strain muddy water and to make a sling, or even a bandage covering. When he pulls it up over his nose it helps keep out dust—fine alkali dust in the nose and lungs can be mighty irritating.

Now take footgear: a cowboy has a very special interest in what he wears on his feet. He will spend a month's wages on a good hand-made pair of boots — and there's a reason. A hundred years of experimenting have gone into them. The toe of the boot is narrow, so that it can slide easily into the stirrup. The high heel keeps a man's foot from slipping all the way through the stirrup. There's *real* trouble if his foot gets caught in the stirrup and he is thrown. The heel of the boot is slanted forward so that the rider's weight rests mostly on the ball of his foot, not on his instep. This way he gets less tired. A cowboy doesn't plan to do much walking in his boots, but they have one good use on the ground. He can dig his high heels into the earth and brace himself when he is afoot, roping a horse out of a remuda.

Cowboy boots are made of the best-grade leather, often French calf, with the flesh side out so the surface won't roughen up or get scratched easily. The boots are usually lined with soft sheep or goat skin. And because a cowboy takes so much interest in them, he often has them decorated. Since they are made to order, he can choose his own favorite art work.

Spurs are another ever-present part of a cowboy's dress. Horsemen have worn them proudly since the days of knighthood, and they are a social requirement for cowboys. But they are also a necessary working tool. A good cowboy rarely uses spurs to punish a horse, but he does use them to guide his mount. And bronc busters find them a mighty handy way of explaining to a horse who's boss.

SADDLES

Two types of Western stock saddle. On the left is the single-rigged California-Nevada saddle. On the right, the double-rigged Texas style. The dally-hold type of roping is used in California and, since this puts less strain on the cinches, a single-rig is adequate. In the Southwest, where the tie-fast hold is used, the greater strain on the cinches requires the double rigging.

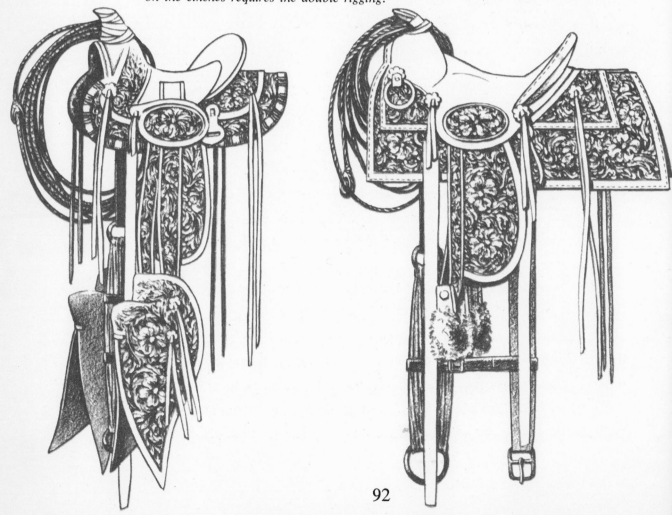

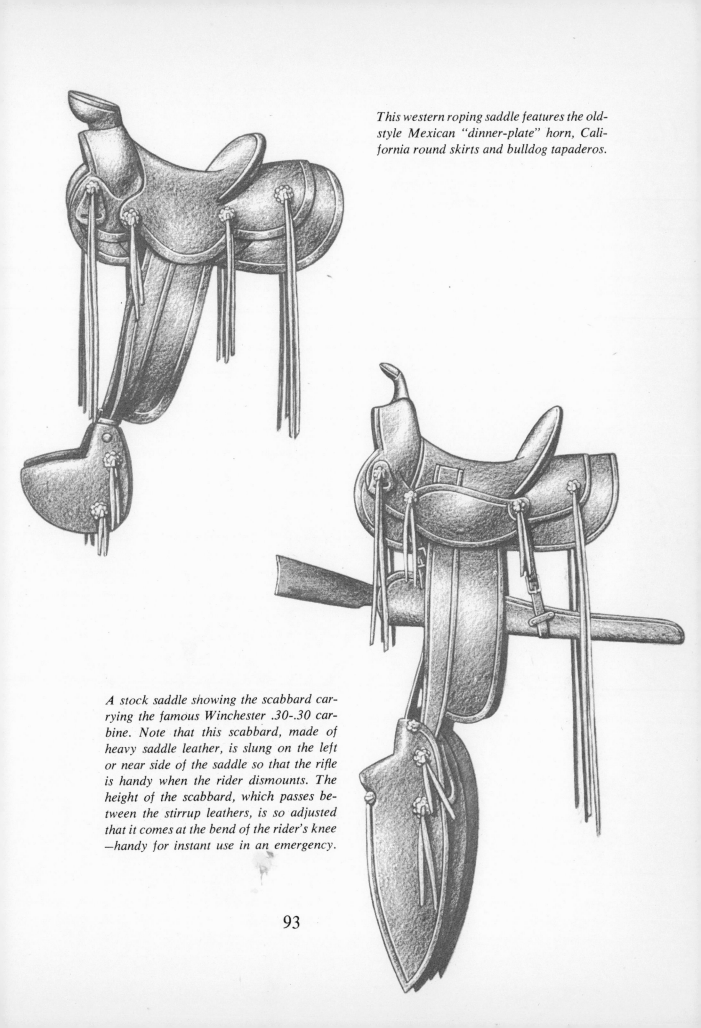

This western roping saddle features the old-style Mexican "dinner-plate" horn, California round skirts and bulldog tapaderos.

A stock saddle showing the scabbard carrying the famous Winchester .30-.30 carbine. Note that this scabbard, made of heavy saddle leather, is slung on the left or near side of the saddle so that the rifle is handy when the rider dismounts. The height of the scabbard, which passes between the stirrup leathers, is so adjusted that it comes at the bend of the rider's knee —handy for instant use in an emergency.

93

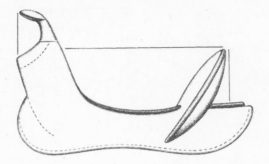

SADDLE TREE MEASUREMENTS

A bad-fitting saddle can cause untold hours of discomfort and plenty of bad language from a working cowhand. For this reason he studies very carefully the measurements of the saddle-tree, knowing that on the accuracy of these measurements depends the comfort of his "work bench" and the efficiency of his work. The tree is the very foundation of the saddle and, unless it is properly made and fitted, the saddle is worthless.

Here are five saddle forks, from the oldest "slick" fork through adaptations of the "bulge" to the modern "swell" fork.

VARIOUS TYPES OF SADDLE HORNS

Mexican "Dinner Plate" Horn   *Leather-Wrapped Horn*   *Duck Bill Horn*   *Sewn Leather-Covered Metal Horn*   *"Slick" Horn*

Low and full slope

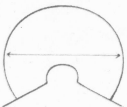

Round type cantle

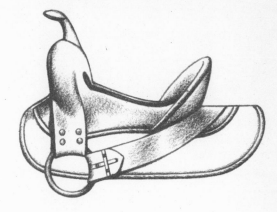

Medium height and slope

Oval type cantle

High and steep slope

In choosing his saddle, the cowboy pays just as much attention to the slope and height of the cantle (back) of the saddle as he does to the horn. In the roping saddle, the cantle is low and has full slope, while in the bronc-busting saddle, the cantle is high and steep sloping.

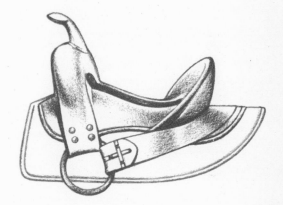

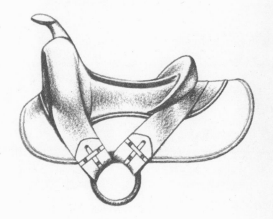

If a saddle ever breaks loose under the strain of roping, the cause is invariably because the saddle rigging gives way. The two main types of rigging are the single and the double. Shown are three adaptations of the single rig: The Spanish rig, the three-quarter rig, and the "center-fire" rig. At the bottom is the double or "rim-fire" rig.

95

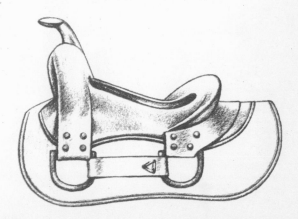

CINCHES

Cinches and latigo straps are the means by which saddles are secured to the backs of horses.

Horsehair cinch. Mane hair is used, not tail hair. Note steel rings.

Mohair cinch, with cadmium rings.

Near (left) side latigo, used for cinching.

Off (right) side (stationary) latigo strap.

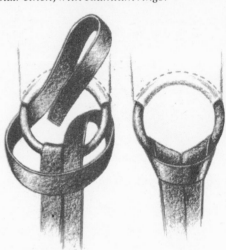

Half-hitch made with latigo in cinching up saddle.

STIRRUPS

Early California wooden stirrup. Note carved out back in rear view.

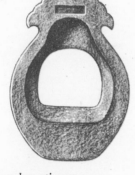

Modern solid-block wooden stirrup.

Galvanized iron bound stirrup, leather top and bottom.

Mexican one-piece solid wood stirrup.

Early Texas box stirrup, iron-bound and very heavy.

Brass-bound ox-bow stirrup, leather top and bottom.

Brass tubular ring stirrup, with leather top.

TAPADEROS

This bull-nose tapadero is often lined with sheep-skin for warmth and dryness.

Monkey-nose tapadero.

Hand-tooled eagle-bill tapadero moulded to fit around stirrup.

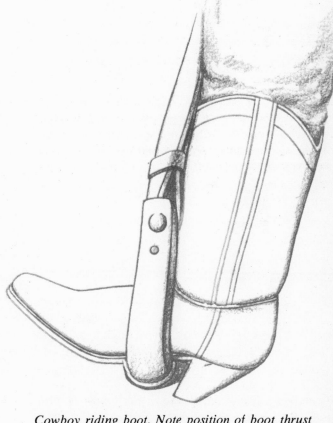

Cowboy riding boot. Note position of boot thrust well forward in the stirrup. The cowboy rides with his weight resting on the reinforced instep of the boot because this is the least tiring position and he expects to spend many hours in the saddle.

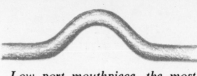

Low port mouthpiece, the most humane type.

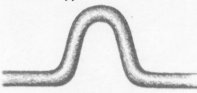

High port mouthpiece.

Half-breed bit with low port.

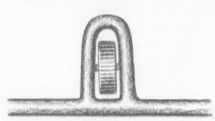

Half-breed bit with high port.

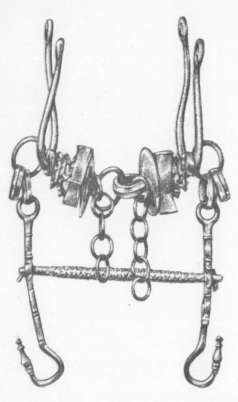

Although the ancient Greeks rode without saddle or stirrups, they could not dispense with bits and, perhaps because there were no other restraints — such as stirrups — the bit pictured above seems to our eyes a very cruel object. Note the attachments which could readily cut the horse's tongue.

Note milled edge wheel, called "cricket" because of the high-pitched noise it gives off when champed by a cow pony.

This ancient Chinese bit, dating to the fourth or fifth century B.C. had a spiked and revolving cover which prevented the horse from getting the bit in his teeth — and, hence, out of control.

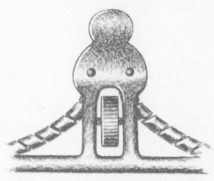

Front view of the low spade mouthpiece, typical of those used on western cow horses.

Side view, full spade bit.

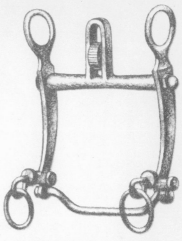

Typical bit used on Western cow horses today. The bar across the bottom is designed to keep the throwing rope from slipping between horse's lip and cheeks of bit when roping.

Breaking bit. This has no mouthpiece but the steel noseband curbs the horse by cutting off his wind at the nostrils.

Old Mexican Chileno or ring bit, hand forged. This is called the "bear trap" bit because it is so cruel to the horse's jaw.

Backview of the Western full-spade bit. Note the braces of wrapped copper wire and the roller or "cricket."

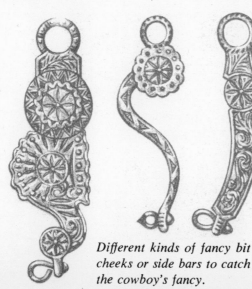

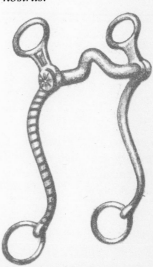

Different kinds of fancy bit cheeks or side bars to catch the cowboy's fancy.

Lightweight racking bit, the sort of bit a cowhand will use when stepping out on his "Sunday horse."

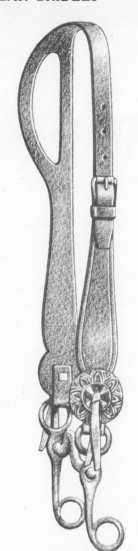

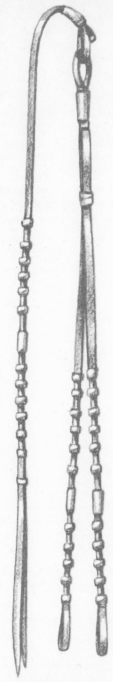

Double ear bridle.

Single ear bridle, with bit laced in.

Texas or split reins are held together by a "keeper."

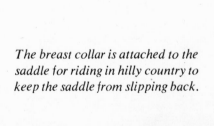

The breast collar is attached to the saddle for riding in hilly country to keep the saddle from slipping back.

California reins, unlike Texas reins, are joined to form a romal, which is used as a quirt.

100

SADDLE BLANKETS

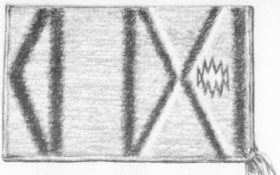

Navajo saddle blanket, made of wool for long wear and easy cleaning.

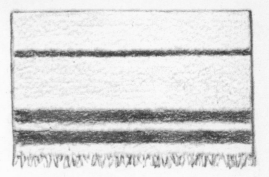

Angora saddle blanket, soft and easy on the horse's back.

SAWBUCK PACK SADDLE

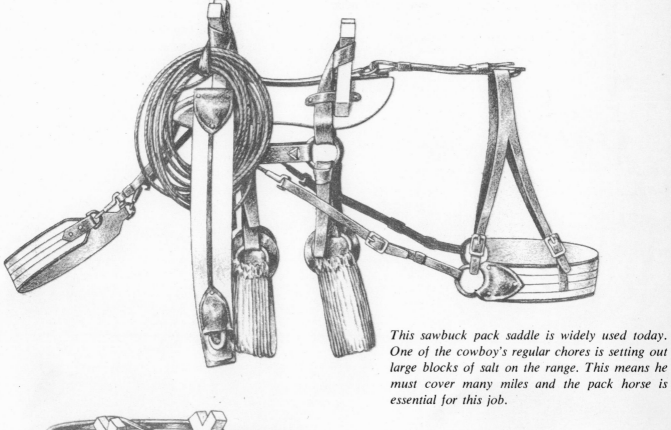

This sawbuck pack saddle is widely used today. One of the cowboy's regular chores is setting out large blocks of salt on the range. This means he must cover many miles and the pack horse is essential for this job.

Pack bags or cantinas made of heavy canvas with harness leather handles and straps.

101

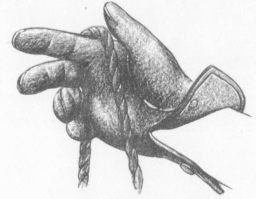

OLD STYLE RAWHIDE HONDA   OVAL BRASS HONDA   EGG SHAPE BRASS HONDA

The honda or eyelet at one end of the rope formerly was made of rawhide woven right in with the rope. Today, hondas are made of metal in one of two styles, oval and egg-shaped. Because it is the point of greatest strain in roping, even the metal honda wears out in time and must be replaced.

Gloves are always worn to prevent rope burn. There is nothing "dudish" about glove wearing. They are worn strictly for self-protection.

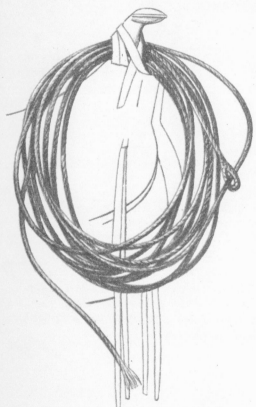

The cowboy's throwing rope is usually carried on the right side of the saddle a little below the horn, coiled in loops about 18" in diameter. This makes the rope easily accessible for uncoiling and throwing with his right hand, while holding the reins with his left.

Cowboy working cuffs made of calfskin, fastened with snaps. These protect the wrists against rope burns and sprains.

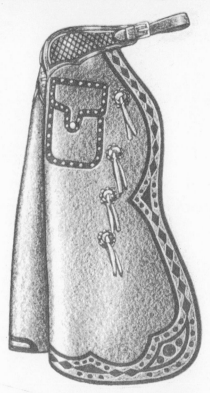

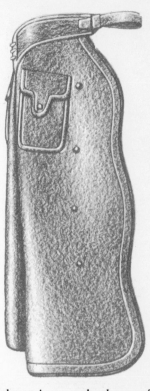

Angora chaps, also called "hair pants," are full, canvas lined and have leather pockets.

Batwing "show" chaps with silver conchas and trimmings are made of tanned calfskin.

Everyday wing work chaps of steerhide are much more rugged than the fancy "show" chaps.

The three standard cuts of chaps.

CHAP BELTS

3 SNAPS AND RINGS

4 SNAPS AND RINGS

5 SNAPS AND RINGS

STRAIGHT

FULL DIP STRAIGHT

CURVED

FULL DIP CURVED

LOW CUT CURVED

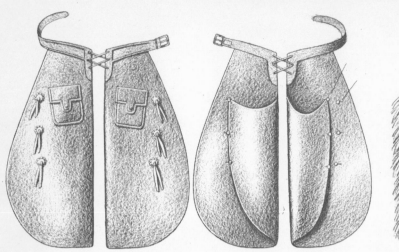

Batwing chaps, front and rear view. These chaps can be removed by loosening the snaps without the cowboy's having to take off his spurs.

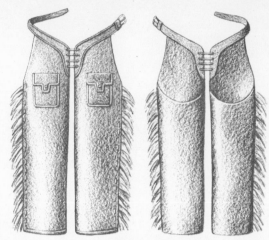

Fringed "shot gun chaps" so called from their resemblance to the twin barrels of a "scatter gun." Because of their closed legs, they cannot be removed without taking off the spurs first. The seams are buckskin laced.

BOOTS

These typical cowboy boots show the elaborate hand-tooling and the bootstraps which old cowhands called "mule ears."

Modern cowboy boots vary in the height of the uppers, the smallest being called "peewees." Many modern boots have colorful designs of dyed leather inlays.

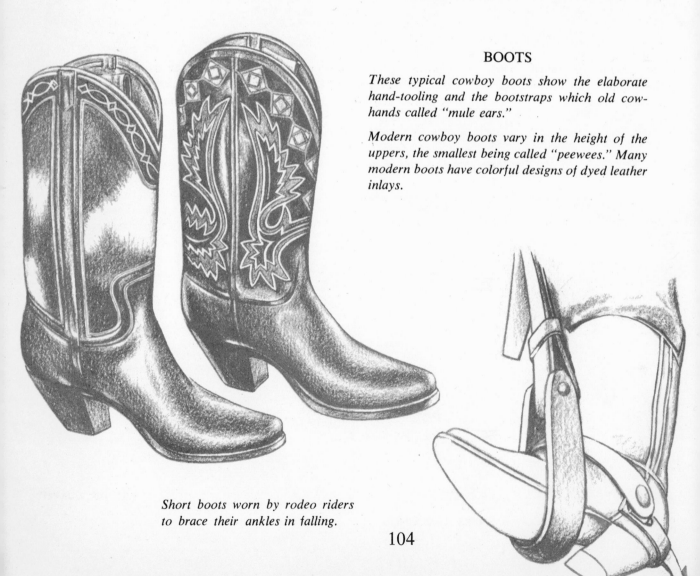

Short boots worn by rodeo riders to brace their ankles in falling.

The Spanish great rowel spur, dating to about 1600 A.D.

Spur attached to boot with the spur leather.

Boxheel rowel spur of the 17th Century.

BUCK HOOK

DANGLERS

Modern California spur. Note the influence of the Spanish great rowel spur. The pear-shaped pendants or "danglers" are purely ornamental but tinkle or, as the cowboy says, "make music while I walk."

Mexican spur of the early 19th Century.

Modern Texas type spur, showing the strong influence of the Mexican spur. Note the buck hook on both these modern spurs. To keep from being thrown, a rider can hook this into the cinch. This is against the rules in official rodeo contests.

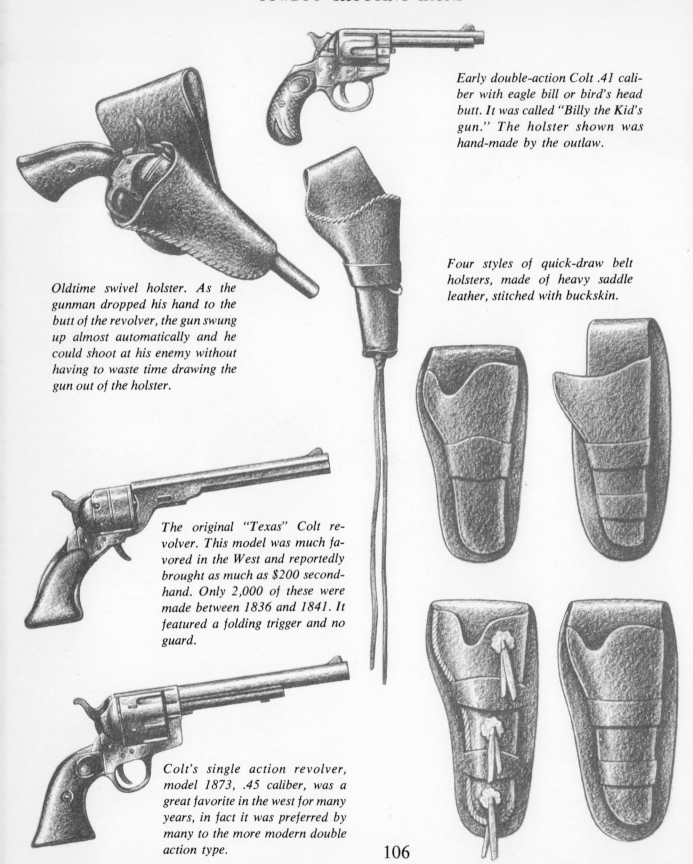

Early double-action Colt .41 caliber with eagle bill or bird's head butt. It was called "Billy the Kid's gun." The holster shown was hand-made by the outlaw.

Oldtime swivel holster. As the gunman dropped his hand to the butt of the revolver, the gun swung up almost automatically and he could shoot at his enemy without having to waste time drawing the gun out of the holster.

Four styles of quick-draw belt holsters, made of heavy saddle leather, stitched with buckskin.

The original "Texas" Colt revolver. This model was much favored in the West and reportedly brought as much as $200 secondhand. Only 2,000 of these were made between 1836 and 1841. It featured a folding trigger and no guard.

Colt's single action revolver, model 1873, .45 caliber, was a great favorite in the west for many years, in fact it was preferred by many to the more modern double action type.

106

THE WINCHESTER REPEATER

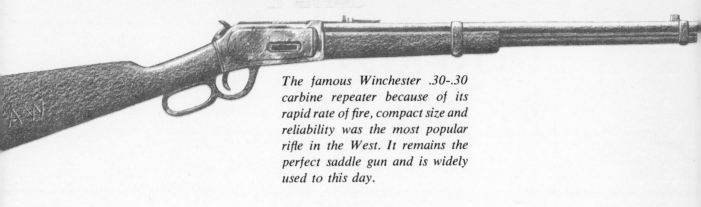

The famous Winchester .30-.30 carbine repeater because of its rapid rate of fire, compact size and reliability was the most popular rifle in the West. It remains the perfect saddle gun and is widely used to this day.

RANGE RIDING TOOLS

Dehorning saw made of special steel. Note the wing nut securing the blade to the handle.

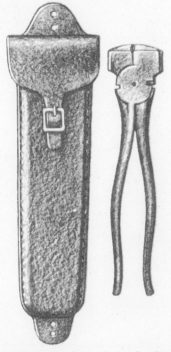

Combination forged steel pliers and hammer used to keep fences in repair. The plier scabbard is made of saddle skirting leather.

Horse hobble with cuffs and swivel chain.

The staple pocket is attached to the cantle of the saddle.

Figure "8" horse hobble made of heavy leather and sheepskin lined. These hobbles are used to let a horse graze at will while preventing him from wandering too far away.

CHAPTER 12

COWBOY RIDING

THIS HAS BEEN MOSTLY ABOUT HOW COWBOYS ride horses that have been gentled. Riding broncs and training them is a story in itself.

Breaking broncs can be done at any time, but it usually begins after the spring roundup is over. Most bronc peelers take four to six weeks to tame an unbroken horse. Some Mexican horse breakers can finish the job in a day or two, but they have to be plenty rough

Any bronc buster who gets spilled can expect a lot of good-natured joshing from the regular ranch hands who watch from the "op'ry house"— the top rail of the breaking corral.

to do it in that time, and they spoil lots of horses. Spoiled horses are outlaws—they never can be tamed.

Sometimes a contract buster goes from ranch to ranch breaking horses, at so much a head. But on most spreads of any size there is usually a bronc twister among the regular hands. He's in charge of the unbroken horses—the rough string.

He does his work in the breaking corral. This is a circular enclosure about eight feet high, made of very strong posts and side rails, all

The Cowboy and His Horse

lashed together securely with lengths of rawhide. Halfway between the center of the corral and the fence is a snubbing post set very firmly in the ground.

Often when a peeler is at work, other hands sit on the top rail of the corral watching the show. This top rail is called the "op'ry house," and the audience isn't a bit bashful about whooping and yelling as the fight between the horse and man goes on. And they poke a lot of good-natured fun at any peeler who is sent picking daisies, which is a cowboy's way of saying bucked off.

"THERE AIN'T A HOSS THAT CAN'T BE RODE; THERE AIN'T A MAN THAT CAN'T BE THROWED."

There are as many ways of breaking horses as there are cowboys. In general, though, this is about the way it works; and the object is always the same—to prove to the horse that a rider is boss:

A peeler goes to a corral where the rough string is kept. He ropes one bronc, takes it into the breaking corral, and turns him loose. Then, with an underhand cast of the rope, he brings the loop up, catching the horse's forelegs. A quick turn of the rope around the snubbing post, and the peeler has the horse held tight. The friction of the rope against the post is as good as a knot.

Now if the horse tries to run, it is thrown by the rope. While it is down, the peeler slips a hackamore over its head and ties one hind foot to a rope around its neck, so that when it gets up it can't put that foot on the ground. This way the horse won't be able to kick when the peeler lets its two front feet free.

When the horse is lying on the ground, the peeler says he is letting it soak. The horse is being told, in a language it understands, that it can no longer do just as it pleases if there is a man around. Once the bronc gets up on three feet, the peeler leads it around the corral. Next he gets it used to having something on its back. He "sacks it out," that is, he touches the bronc's back with a sack. After the horse gets used

QUIRT

110

to the sack, the cowboy puts a saddle on for a moment, then takes it off. He keeps on until the horse is used to the saddle and will let it stay on. All this may go on for as long as several weeks before the peeler decides the horse is ready to be ridden. But he doesn't expect a nice easy ride when he climbs aboard. He is ready for action and he usually gets it.

Cowboy Riding

Not until the bronc has become used to the feel of a saddle does the "peeler" climb aboard — and when he does, he's ready for a rough, bucking ride.

The bronc starts to buck in an effort to dislodge the unfamiliar weight on his back. The peeler tries not to be bucked — he wants to stay the boss all the time. When the horse finally gets tired of bucking he starts to run, and the peeler lets him for a while. This is what he has been working up to.

Western gun-fighters were known to make a notch in the butt of their revolvers every time they killed a man. For this reason a man-killer bronc is sometimes said to have "a notch in his tail."

The horse may still buck when it is mounted the next time, but now the peeler can start topping it off. He trains it to accept a bridle and to get used to a bit in its mouth. He teaches it to turn to the left when a rein touches the right side of its neck. The horse gradually learns to respond to pressure of the rider's heels and knees. It is ready now to go out on the range and learn how to work with cattle.

Cowboy Riding

Taming a horse requires not only quick action at times, but a great deal of patience as well. It's possible to break a horse without having it buck at all, but that takes more time than a cowboy usually has. Indian horses in the early days almost never bucked, because their riders didn't have to be in a hurry about getting the mustangs ready to ride. They had time enough in which to win the animal's confidence and get them used to being around people. The Indians, too, sacked out, but they added an extra step. They spent hours just leaning with their arms over their horses' backs. Gradually the mustangs became accustomed to the feel of a human body and its pressure on their skins. When an Indian finally put all his weight on a horse's back, it was no surprise, and so the mustang didn't boil over. A horse broken in this long, slow way was said to be "Indian gentled."

The Cowboy and His Horse

with a lot of smaller hazards in his day-to-day work. Rattlesnakes, for instance. A rattler's bite can make cattle or horses very sick, although it seldom kills them. It can come mighty near to killing a grown man and sometimes does.

Cattle and horses, too, can break their legs in prairie-dog holes and badger holes. More than one cowboy has been set afoot because his horse "threw a foot" in the burrow of one of these prairie animals. On the range a horse with a broken leg has to be killed. Shooting a good cow horse to end its misery is something no waddie likes to do. A skunk is another four-legged pest in some parts, and not just because of its smell. Although the skunk has its uses—it kills gophers and moles and field mice—it sometimes carries hydrophobia, and if a skunk with hydrophobia bites a sleeping cowboy he gets the dread disease. This only happens once in a very long while, but skunks are night prowlers and they do get into camps and chew up latigos and parts of saddles to get at the salt in the leather, which comes from horses' sweat. That's bad business, because a cowboy doesn't carry a load of spare parts with him every time he's out on the range.

When the fall roundup is over and winter sets in, regular hands on the ranch still have plenty of work to do—and in all kinds of weather.

116

A colt is easy prey for the mountain lion, lying in wait at the water hole.

*Range
Riders*

A real "norther" can make the cowhand's life miserable. Not only must he make every effort to head full-grown cattle into shelter but he must frequently saddle-pack a calf back to a safe corral to save it from freezing.

Beginning in the fall, cold winds called northers plague the Texas cowboys. A norther can make the temperature fall thirty or forty degrees in a few hours. Although it rarely goes more than a few degrees below freezing, old cattle or weak stock often die. A cowboy's job is to get stock into sheltered places.

On the plains farther north, cowboys and cattle have to face blizzards. The wind often thunders over the plains at fifty miles an hour, driving sleet or snow with it. Drifts pile up, and the temperature drops below zero. Any living thing, caught in the open by the blasts of a real Western blizzard, is certain to perish.

Often just the opposite happens. A peculiar kind of warm wind, called a chinook, sweeps down over the northern ranges when they are covered with snow. A chinook melts the snow almost overnight.

117

The Cowboy and His Horse

Now the cattle can get at the grass, but the sudden change in temperature also weakens some of them. They lie down and never get up unless a cowboy prods them to their feet.

On big spreads, cowboys often live in pairs in small cabins out on the range during the winter. They make daily rides to look out for weak or sick cattle. These they bring into a hospital pen near the

The rattlesnake is one of many range menaces—though not feared as much by cowhands as you might expect. Matter of fact, most cowpokes feel the rattlers come in handy because they provide a fine excuse for gun practice.

cabin where they have shelter and good hay. The cowboys also take hay out onto the ranges when snow keeps cattle from getting enough grass.

It gets plenty lonesome for the two cowpokes out on the range. They are cut off from their home spread, sometimes for a month or two at a time. Many a deck of cards has been worn to a frazzle in a

118

tiny one-room shack twenty or thirty or more miles from the nearest neighbor.

For every cowboy who is cooking his own flapjacks and beans and coffee out on the range, there is another riding the chuck line looking for a new job. A few hang around the cow towns or big cities as long as their money lasts. Some take jobs in Hollywood riding in cowboy pictures. But there are fewer and fewer wandering cowboys these days. Many live all year round with their families right on the spread where they work.

A tragic aftermath of severe blizzards are dozens — sometimes hundreds — of "die-ups." These are cattle who, trying to flee the storm, become caught in the wire fence and die of cold and starvation. Usually their carcasses have been stripped by wolves or coyotes before they are found.

CHAPTER 14

COWBOY DANCE

THERE ARE PLENTY OF HEADACHES on the range in summer, but there is fun too. After the spring roundup, ranch hands light out for the nearest cow town and a good time. Or they may get together for cowboy square dances, just as they did a hundred years ago. There are more women around in cow country these days, so the practice of heifer-branding half the cowboys has gone out of fashion. But a fiddler still twangs away and there may be a guitar or an accordion as well.

With the fiddler sawing out the tune, and the caller singing out calls for the various figures, the dance gets under way, and it's likely to last the whole night. Here's one favorite:

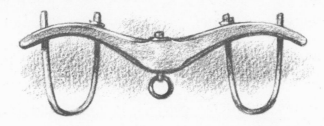

GET YO' LITTLE SAGEHENS READY

Get yo' little sagehens ready, Trot 'em out upon the floor.

Line up there, you cusses! Steady! Lively, now. One couple more.

Shorty, shed that old sombrero! Broncho, douse that cigaret;

Stop that cussin', Casimero, 'Fore the ladies! Now, all set!

S'lute your ladies, all together!
Ladies opposite the same —
Hit the lumber with your leathers!
Balance all, an' swing your dame!

Gents to center, ladies 'round 'em,
Form a basket, balance all!
Whirl yer girls to where you found 'em;
Promenade around the hall!

Balance to yer pards an' trot 'em.
'Round the circle double quick,
Grab an' kiss while you've got 'em,
Hold 'em to it if they kick!

First four forward! Back to places!
Second fellow, shuffle back!
Now you've got it down to cases —
Swing 'em till their trotters crack!

Gents all right a'heel an' toeing!
Swing 'em, kiss 'em if you kin —
On to next and keep a-goin',
Till yer hit yer pards agin!

Ladies, left hand to your sonnies!
Alaman! Grand right an' left!
Balance all an' swing yer honeys —
Pick 'em up an' feel their heft!

Promenade like skeery cattle —
Balance all an' swing yer sweets!
Shake yer spurs an' make 'em rattle!
Keno! Promenade to seats.

CHAPTER 15

THE OLD
AND THE NEW

NO TWO RANCHES HAVE EVER BEEN EXACTLY ALIKE,
but nowadays they differ from each other more and more every year.
Some big spreads are run pretty much the way they were fifty or a
hundred years ago. Others are as different from old-time spreads as
a fleet of trucks from a remuda on a roundup. Small ranches have
changed even more than big ones. They have had to use all kinds of
modern scientific inventions in order to make out at all.

The Cowboy and His Horse

The interesting thing is that science has helped to keep one colorful side of old-time cowboy life alive. Every year, cattle drives roll across New Mexico, bawling and stirring up clouds of dust as they did in the days of the Chisholm Trail. This is the story.

Many small ranchers needed to run more cattle than their pastures could feed. There were more pastures available, owned by the government, but cattle had to have some way of getting from the home ranch to the government grazing land. So the United States Grazing Service worked out a plan. It mapped and organized the great Magdalena driveway for cattle (and sheep) which almost 400 ranchers can use.

Science rules the driveway. There are speed limits for the herds that use it. Cattle and horses must travel at least ten miles a day toward the new pastures. Government overseers act as traffic cops and make sure that herds move fast enough so they won't eat up all the grass on the driveway, leaving none for the herds that follow. Windmills fill water holes or "tanks" at intervals. Corrals have been built along the way so that night herding is seldom necessary.

In spite of all these conveniences, cowpokes still haze the cattle over the trail in the old way. And they still need to have cowboy savvy about the critters they are driving along

Science and invention have changed life on many ranches. Here are some of the things that go on today.

Nearly all critters, from calves on up, are "spooky." This means that they can be easily frightened by an unusual sound or, as in this case, by the appearance of an unfamiliar though harmless tortoise.

124

Cowboys sometimes use jeeps and pick-up trucks instead of horses for driving cattle. They've learned to be assistant veterinarians, giving injections against disease. Instead of wearing six-shooters on their hips, they're likely to use spray-guns filled with chemicals to kill ticks.

Instead of singing "Oh, Bury Me Not on the Lone Prairie" as he rides night herd, a cowpoke may be lying in his bunk listening to the song over the radio. He's had to learn the uses of a monkey wrench as well as a lariat, for he often repairs windmills and other modern equipment. He knows not only how to shoe a horse but how to change truck tires and how to breed and rear prize bulls.

In the old days cowboys used to bring in firewood for the cook by roping a bunch of mesquite and dragging it along tied to the saddle horn. Now, machines clear the mesquite and chaparral from pastures, in order to make more grazing land for cattle. Sometimes a machine like a steam shovel clamps down over the bushes and pulls them up. Or two tractors may clear a pasture with a chain which they drag between them.

There are spreads where a cowboy rides in the saddle all day, then flies back to the ranch headquarters at night in a plane which comes to pick him up. And at the ranch house he has a meal cooked on an electric range. Afterwards he may drive an auto into town to see a western at the movies.

AIRPLANES ON THE MODERN RANCH

Airplanes have other uses, too. A few years ago when a great blizzard struck most of the range in the West, planes delivered hay to cattle that were marooned without food. This was known as "Operation Haylift." In snow-covered Nevada, Arizona, Colorado and other parts of cow country, bales of hay plunged down out of the sky and burst open when they landed, saving the lives of countless animals.

On one ranch, at least, cowpokes heat their branding irons in a

Just a few years ago the United States Air Force cooperated with ranchers in Nevada and Colorado to get hay to thousands of range cattle marooned by blizzards. Called "Operation Haylift," it is credited with saving the lives of many large herds.

flame that comes from bottled gas. Many ranchers have tried to use chemicals instead of hot irons for branding. That hasn't worked well yet, but on some spreads a new method has speeded up the branding process. Instead of roping and hog-tieing calves, cowboys drive the calves into corrals and then, one by one, into what is called a squeeze pen. This is simply a crate with movable sides that can be pushed together against the calf, holding it motionless. All a cowboy has to do is shove the branding iron between the slats in the crate. An inoculating needle can be poked into the animal at the same time.

The usual place for branding is the left hip, but one rancher in Wyoming tried dabbing his large brand on the backs of his critters, because he could look after them better that way when he flew around over the range in his private plane. He could tell where his cattle were grazing by looking down from above and seeing their brands.

So many people have been interested in cowboys that they have wanted to spend their vacations on ranches. Hundreds of ranches have taken in paying guests. City people come out and dress and ride and eat like cowboys. The hands call the guests "dudes," and the spreads where they stay are "dude ranches." Cowboys whose job it is to herd the city folk around are called "dude wranglers."

Dude wrangling is one of the new special jobs which a cowpoke can take on if he wants to. He may ride in a rodeo, put on specially for the guests, or take them camping, or he may join them in cowboy dances and sing cowboy songs. Whatever he does, he has to know horses and how to handle them in the old way.

The Old and The New

CHAPTER 16

RODEOS—
WEST AND EAST

IT'S A LONG WAY FROM A CORRAL on a ranch to the big indoor arena at Madison Square Garden in New York City. But rodeos began under the blazing sun in dusty corrals, with the audience perched on the "op'ry house" rail to watch buckaroos in action, and they have ended up under electric lights where ten or fifteen thousand people can watch at one time.

Coming out of chute number 6 in a western rodeo, this saddle bronc contestant is fighting hard to stay on his plunging, bucking mount. Note the "pick up" man in the rear. His job is to head the bronc away from the sprawling rider if he gets thrown.

Rodeos— West and East

All sections of the country have rodeos now, the East as well as the West. More people go to rodeos than to any other outdoor sports events except baseball. Every year about ten million Americans turn out for the saddle bronc riding and wild horse racing and steer wrestling and the clowns and stunts that make up a rodeo. And the interest in rodeos has spread outside the United States. Cowboys travel to Europe to show their skill. There are even rodeos now on the other side of the world in which Australian cowboys try to stay aboard Australian broncs.

The Cowboy and His Horse

Now the rodeo is a great show, but back in the days when it started there was very little of the circus about it. Only cowboys came to watch other "saddle stiffs" perform. Mexican vaqueros and American cowhands were proud of their skill in the saddle and each of them wanted to show the others how good he was.

In the early days Mexican riders in Texas and California often had contests at the fiestas, or celebrations, which followed roundups. The Spanish word for roundup is *rodeo* and that's where the name for the contests came from. It's pronounced either roh-*day*-o, or *roh*-dee-oh. Cowhands who followed the vaqueros got the rodeo habit from them. In places where the fiesta was not traditional the contests were often held right on a ranch after the work was done.

Men from one outfit bet money, if they had any, that their top roper could put a loop on a calf's neck and hog-tie it more quickly than the top roper on a neighboring spread. They bet on who could stay in the saddle longest on some outlaw bronc. They bet on who would be the first to rope a running jack rabbit.

Like old-time miners in the West who held rock-drilling contests, cowboys competed among themselves. And like the miners, they often had their big contests on the Fourth of July. The independent people on the frontier had a special liking for Independence Day. It was important to them. It also came at a time when most cowboys were through with the spring roundup. They had been paid off and wanted to cut loose and have some fun.

It was a while before prizes were given at rodeos. That didn't happen until 1883 in Pecos, Texas. After that other rodeos on different parts of the range began to offer prizes. For instance, there was a rodeo the next year, 1884, up north close to the Canadian border at Fort Benton, Montana, where prizes were given. The

A favorite stunt in the old-time Texas rodeos was roping jack rabbits. This contest required skill, speed and an unerring eye.

130

highest was $50. Spring came later in Montana than in Texas, so this rodeo wasn't held until late in July.

INDIANS AND MOUNTIES COME TO WATCH

Everybody for miles around Fort Benton came to watch. There were bull whackers, the men who drove teams of oxen pulling covered wagons over the Oregon trail — or some other trail. Red-coated Canadian Mounted Police, most of them former cowboys, came across the border from Canada. Blackfeet Indians and Piegan Indians were there, decked out in feather war-bonnets and paint for a celebration. Trappers came in from the wilderness. Mule skinners left their creak-

ing prairie schooners to join the crowd, and stage-coach drivers came along with their passengers. Women traveled up the Missouri River by steamboat to join the fun. Soldiers from a nearby fort came with their band. They had all heard there was going to be a "Grand Riding and Racing Contest Celebrating the Close of the Judith Basin and Shonkin Roundup."

The whole affair started with a parade. Some people were ready for it at sunrise — that is the time when almost everybody got up anyway. Indians put feathers in the manes and tails of their best ponies. Soldiers rode their cavalry mounts, sitting differently in their saddles from the way cowboys sat. The Canadian Mounted Police — and everyone else in the parade — rode eight abreast. All the riders, and most of those who watched them, had six-shooters on their hips.

A REAL OLD-TIME RODEO

After the parade the crowd gathered outside of town in open flat country. There was no grandstand and no fenced-in place for the contests, and many of the contests went on all at once. Sometimes there were twenty-five cowboys riding bucking broncos and twenty-five others roping steers at the same time. Chinese laborers, smartly dressed gamblers, new settlers, leathery old cowboys — all stood in the crowd watching. It was a grand mix-up. And on the evening of the first day of the celebration two huge steers were barbecued.

That was an old-time rodeo. Nobody paid to see it. As a matter of fact, no admission was charged at any rodeo until 1888 at Prescott, Arizona, but since then the custom has spread. Now there are 225 big rodeos every year, and many more smaller ones. There is the Frontier Day celebration at Cheyenne, Wyoming — which calls itself the "Daddy of 'Em All." Canada has the Calgary Stampede. The Navajo Indians, some of whom are great cowboys, have two rodeos every year. And in Tucson, Arizona, there is La Fiesta de los Vaqueros.

132

"Sunning his moccasins" is the old-time phrase describing a bronc rider who has just been thrown. It probably can be traced back to when the original cow hunters of Texas and Mexico wore moccasins.

Eastern cities have rodeos too. They have been going on there since 1916 when the first one was held in Brooklyn. Most of these rodeos now are held for cowboys who make their living from rodeos rather than from work on ranches. That goes even for small rodeos

The Cowboy and His Horse

held each week on dude ranches. But no professional can ride in the annual rodeo at Stamford, Texas. It's for home folks only.

There's another very unusual rodeo every year at Dallas, Texas, where the contestants are prison inmates — cowboys who have got in trouble with the law. As they fork outlaw broncs, they wear their striped prison clothes between their ten-gallon cowboy hats and high-heeled cowboy boots — and they show plenty of courage. These cow-

According to rodeo contest rules a rider has to "come out scratching." This means that he must leave the chute with his boots on the horse's shoulders and rake his feet back and forth as long as he stays aboard or until the whistle sounds.

134

boys in jail won't stand for any cheating, either. And when they win prizes they send the money home, if they have a home.

From the beginning cowboys have paid entrance fees to take part in rodeos. They did this way back when some rodeos were called Cowboy Tournaments. They do it now, and there are rodeos going ten months in the year. They begin in September and end with the World Championship Rodeo in Madison Square Garden in New York in September.

Any good rider or roper has a chance in the show, whether he grew up on a ranch or not. Harry Tompkins, the World Champion Cowboy for 1948 and 1949, was born near New York and never saw a western ranch until he was seventeen. Out of the old sport, which came from the joy which cowboys took in their work, has grown a great national sport in which any daring athlete can take part — if he knows horses and ropes, and a few other things.

UNUSUAL EVENTS IN EARLY RODEOS

In the beginning there were no rules particularly. You rode a bronc until he threw you or until he gave up. Now the contest lasts ten seconds — and a long ten seconds it is for the rider. The rules favor the horse. Those who run rodeos know it makes a better show this way.

In the early days in California, cowboys ran races to see who would be first in pulling off the heads of chickens that had been buried in the ground with only the head showing. Farther east, contestants often tried to rope jack rabbits. Indian women had relay races at some rodeos. And there were often regular horse races between cowboys, too. There was all kinds of excitement. You see, ranch people were lonely most of the year, and they enjoyed getting together with other people. They enjoyed seeing who was best at some of the jobs cowboys have to do, and there was extra fun watching stunts which only cowboys could think of.

THE WORLD'S

*The greatest event of the year for the professional rodeo rider is, of course,
the World's Championship Rodeo at Madison Square Garden in New York
City. This is the "big one" where the national championships are decided and
the biggest prizes awarded.*

136

CHAMPIONSHIP RODEO

In the foreground, a championship rider is riding "high, wide and handsome" and is near the end of his ten-second ride in the saddle bronc contest. In the background, note the judge carefully scoring the performances of both rider and horse.

The Cowboy and His Horse

And there is fun today. Rodeo cowboys have become experts by long practice, and, whether or not they come from a ranch, they have learned a great deal from cowboys who did. The working cowboys on the range were the ones who discovered how to make a figure-eight loop in a rope, how to tie a calf's feet quickly with a piggin string, and how to keep balance on the hurricane deck of a bucking outlaw.

This rider has just been sent "picking daisies" by a bronc which is "swapping ends"— that is, turning end for end while in mid-air.

Cowboys are not the only ones who have learned these tricks. Cowgirls have learned them too. In many rodeos there is even a cowgirls' saddle bronc riding contest. And stunt riding, like the riding in circuses, helps make rodeos interesting. Sometimes a rider will ride two bareback horses at the same time standing with one foot on each. The rider and his two horses may even jump over an automobile that is driven into the arena. All these are just stunts and not part of the regular rodeo contests.

These contests are definite and they have definite rules. Here are the five standard rodeo events which almost every rodeo has, and some rodeos have many more: bull or steer riding; bareback bronc riding; bulldogging or steer wrestling; calf roping; and saddle bronc riding. These are the five main events, but there may be wild horse racing, wild cow milking, steer roping and other events as well.

HOW CHAMPIONS ARE CHOSEN

Judges watch all the events carefully and give points to each contestant. The winner in each event, of course, is the one with the most points, or the best time. He gets the prize money. And at the end of the rodeo season the cowboy who has won the most prize money is declared to be all-round champion.

Each event has special rules which are approved by the Rodeo Cowboy Association — an organization that has over two thousand members. Most rodeo fans don't realize how complicated these rules are, so very often they don't fully appreciate the skill and daring that have gone into one brief ride on a bronc or one quick tussle with a steer. You really ought to know at least the most important of these rules.

For instance, in the steer riding contest the steers are Brahmas — a cross between the big sacred cow of India and the wild longhorns of Texas. All the rider has to hold onto is a rope passed loosely around

The Cowboy and His Horse

the steer's middle, and the rider can use only one hand on that. Just to be sure the steer will be in fighting mood and ready to buck, a noisy cowbell is tied to the rope under the steer's belly, and a buck-strap is tightened about the steer's belly just in front of his rear legs.

This burly Brahma steer has just thrown his rider in the bull riding contest — considered by most contestants the most rugged rodeo event.

Each rider draws his steer by lot and he has to be ready when the judges call on him. If he is not ready, he is disqualified. A cowboy has to have his spurs up on the steer's shoulders when he comes out of the chute, and he has to keep "scratching" with them during the ride — that is, he has to keep spurring to make sure the steer will buck.

This event lasts only ten seconds but many cowboys say it is the hardest and most dangerous of all the events. And the danger is not over when the contestant hears the judges' bell announcing that he should dismount. The steer is very likely to charge the rider and try to gore him. There are big knobs on the ends of his horns to protect cowboys from this, but an angry Brahma can still do plenty of damage and that's why there are always clowns around when steer riding is going on. They aren't there just to make you laugh, although they are as good as circus clowns at doing that. Their real job is to draw the attention of the steer away from the rider after he has dismounted or been thrown.

The clowns sometimes do this by throwing a dummy in the steer's way, or they may wave something in front of the steer, or run across his path. One clown may even stand in front of a barrel and tease a steer until he charges. Then the clown jumps into the barrel, which is strong enough to take the shock when the steer crashes into it.

BAREBACK BRONC RIDING

Rules for the bareback bronc riding contest are just about the same as for steer riding. There is a surcingle, or broad leather band, around the horse's belly, and there are leather loops on the surcingle. A cowboy holds one of these loops with one hand and has to hold the other up away from the horse. When a rider dismounts he tries to leap off so that he lands on both feet with his back to the bronc. It is much safer not to be facing the flying heels of a frenzied bronc. And in the bareback bronc riding contest there are no clowns or other riders around to come to his rescue.

BULLDOGGING OR STEER WRESTLING

This exciting event is newer in rodeo than many of the others. The first time it was part of a regular show was in 1907 when a Negro cowboy named Bill Picket showed what he could do to a steer barehanded.

141

The Cowboy and His Horse

It was a while before other cowboys decided to imitate him, but they gradually got the knack of bulldogging, or steer wrestling as it is called in some states. Now it is a part of most rodeos, but in California steer decorating takes its place. In this contest the object is not to throw a steer, but merely to put a big rubber ring over the steer's muzzle.

This contestant in the steer wrestling event has almost dogged his steer to the ground. He is allowed only two minutes to accomplish this tremendous feat.

Although bulldogging is fairly new as a contest, the term "bulldogging" is very old in this country. It comes from the South, where, in early days, special bull dogs were trained to throw steers or bulls. To throw a steer a dog leaped up, fastened its teeth in the animal's muzzle, and then shook its body back and forth. It wasn't long until the steer was on its side ready for branding. Cowboys in the West found it was easier to throw cattle by using their lariats, and it was of course better for the cattle, too. Cowboys today never use dogs to throw cattle, and on the range they almost never wrestle steers barehanded. That's an event for rodeos only.

142

Here's how the contest goes. A steer is driven into a chute on an edge of the arena. The wrestler, or "dogger," sits on his horse to one side of the chute, and an assistant or hazer is in the saddle on the other side of the chute. At a signal the steer is released and both dogger and hazer dash after him across a deadline. The hazer rides close to the steer and keeps him as close as possible to the dogger. When the dogger has crossed the deadline and is even with the steer's flank he dives headlong toward the running steer and grabs his horns. Holding them tight, the dogger gives great leaps in the air as the animal races along pulling him.

As soon as he can, the dogger throws his right arm over the steer's neck and grabs the base of the steer's right horn. Then he holds the tip of the steer's left horn with his left hand and jumps into the air, coming down with all his weight on his left hand. At the same time he pulls up as hard as he can with his right hand. With his horns being used as a lever this way the steer begins to lose his balance. If the dogger is clever, it is no time before the steer's nose is pointing straight up to the sky and the huge animal is flat on his side on the ground. The moment the steer is down, the dogger throws one arm up in the air. The scorer, seeing this, swings down a flag he is holding and time is counted. Now the hazer catches the dogger's horse and he also helps the clowns protect the dogger from the steer.

CALF ROPING

Cowboys on the range still do plenty of roping, and a calf roping contest is part of every rodeo. The winner is the cowboy who can rope a calf, throw it to the ground, and tie its feet together in the shortest time. A calf is let out of a chute and given a thirty foot head start. Then a cowboy on his horse dashes after the calf, his rope swinging with a loop open ready to drop over the calf's head. When the loop falls in place, the horse comes to a stop. He has been very carefully trained and he usually stops gradually, leaving the calf standing. The rules

The Cowboy and His Horse

say if a calf is "busted," that is thrown off his feet, the contestant is fined ten seconds. In other words he has ten seconds added to whatever his actual time is.

If the loop in the rope is too big, and the calf runs through, or too small and misses the calf's head, the contestant is allowed to make one more cast. When he has made a good cast the cowboy dismounts, leaving the rope tied to the saddle horn. By facing the calf and backing away from it, the horse keeps this rope taut. Going hand over hand down the rope, the contestant runs to the calf. Then he "flanks" it. He reaches over the calf's back and under the calf's belly and grabs the legs closest to him. Now he heaves up, throwing the calf off balance and down on its side with the kicking feet away from the contestant.

All the time the cowboy has been carrying a piggin string, or small rope, in his mouth or through his belt. In a flash he has this rope around three feet and tied in a square knot. The instant the knot is tied, the

This roper has nearly completed tying up the calf's legs in the calf roping contest. Note how his well-trained horse keeps the rope taut.

144

cowboy raises a hand. The time keeper marks down the time and judges inspect the knot. All this, from the time the calf starts running until he is hog-tied takes only twenty seconds or less, if the contestant is a top roper.

SADDLE BRONC RIDING

Most of the champion ropers have come from the Southwest — the part of the country in which roping was first used. But that's not true of saddle bronc riders. Most of the champions have come from north of Colorado. Wherever they come from and wherever they compete, the rules are the same. They draw horses by lot. They must ride with only a plain halter — no bit — and only one rein. They must hold one hand in the air during the whole ride, and they have to come out of the chute with spurs on the bronc's neck and keep scratching, backwards and forwards, as they ride.

Every contestant has exactly the same kind of saddle — an "Association" saddle provided by those who run the rodeos. A contestant is not supposed to wrap the rein around his hand. He cannot grab the saddle horn or "pull leather." He is disqualified if he is bucked off, or if a foot slips out of a stirrup, or if he "coasts"— that is rides all the way with his feet on the horse's shoulders. He can't change hands on the rein and he is forbidden to pull the horse's head down with the rein. There always has to be "daylight showing" between the rein and neck. There's a lot of things to remember when a bronc boils over.

The rules favor the horse and the judges give points both to the horse and the rider. If a horse doesn't buck very hard, it counts against the rider, even if he stays in the saddle for the regulation ten seconds. That sounds like a short time, but a real outlaw will make twenty or thirty bucks in that time. And the first few bucks usually tell the story. Most contestants who are sent picking daisies land in the dust after the first or second buck.

Saddle bronc riding is the most important contest in rodeo. The

145

The Cowboy and His Horse

biggest prizes are offered for the winners, and the winners have to be good. No two horses buck the same way — each has his own combination of ways to shake a rider off his back. But there are many kinds of bucks that are well known and easily recognized. A "crow hop" is the easiest buck. Cow horses on the range often crow hop a little on frosty mornings. This buck is really only a gallop done to a kind of jazz rhythm. The horse puts one foot down out of the regular order, and a rider who is not alert can be joggled out of the saddle by this unexpected motion.

A "pile driver" on the other hand is a terrific buck. The horse jumps into the air and comes down stiff legged, giving the rider a heavy jolt.

When a horse gives a sharp turn or twist after he has jumped into the air, the buck may be a "side winder." When a horse turns all the way around he "swaps ends."

"Sunfishing" is the motion a horse makes when he raises his forelegs off the ground, then leaps forward and lands with one shoulder much lower than the other. On this buck the horse tries to heave the rider forward out of the saddle — and to one side or the other.

Some broncs aren't satisfied with bucks like these. They actually try to kill their riders by rearing back and falling on them. When a horse tries this "fall back," a rider has to leave the saddle in a hurry or be crushed. Some horses will even kill themselves in their frenzy to get rid of a rider. A horse like this is called a blind bucker. He may run straight into a fence and break his neck.

Yes, bronc riding is dangerous work. Cowboys who do it have to keep in perfect physical condition, just the way other professional athletes do. And cowboys also take special precautions against injury

Special supporting belt worn by some bronc busters.

Bareback bronc riding.

Rodeos—West and East

when they are in the saddle. Many wear special broad belts to protect their insides from being hurt by the awful jolts they take while aboard a bronc. And cowboys have little tricks like placing their saddles a little farther back on a bronc than they do when riding a broken horse on the range. They say the horse's spine has more "give" or bend at this point. That little bit of springiness helps.

A good rodeo cowboy knows all these tricks and many others. He needs to know them for he is taking part in one of the world's most dangerous sports — and he has to pay all his own hospital bills. He needs all the knowledge about rough horses that cowboys have gathered ever since they first began to round up mustangs and then ride them while driving great herds of longhorns. He learns from the experience of all the cowboys who have ever forked horses.

And all these cowboys together have written one of the most colorful pages in the dramatic history of our country.

147

RODEO ROUNDUP

The Cowboy and His Horse

Every summer and fall, hundreds of towns and cities throughout the Midwest and Canada hold rodeos, most of them under the rules of the Rodeo Cowboys Association. Here is a list of some of the most famous rodeos, together with the month in which they are usually held. If you want more specific dates, just write to the Chamber of Commerce in the town and you'll soon have all the information you want. There's just no more exciting way to spend a day than at one of these real ripsnortin' jamborees.

ARIZONA

July: Prescott, Flagstaff, Springerville, Show Low, St. Johns
September: Benson, Williams

ARKANSAS

June: Fayetteville
July: Springdale
August: Magnolia
September: Russelville, Hope

CALIFORNIA

June: Eureka, Jackson, San Juan Bautista, Salinas, Pleasanton, Del Mar
July: Calistoga, Willits, Galt, Fortuna
August: Ferndale, Roseville, Quincy, Napa, Woodland, Gridley, Paso Robles, Fresno, Los Angeles, Northridge, Sacramento
September: Bishop, McArthur, Mariposa, Anderson, Cedarville, Orland, Merced, Guadalupe, Auburn, Madera, Yuba City
October: Ventura, Hanford, Mojave, San Francisco

COLORADO

June: Greeley
July: Steamboat Springs, Woodland Park
August: Monte Vista, Durango, Evergreen, Estes Park, Colorado Springs, Akron, Longmont, Pueblo

IDAHO

June: Rigby, Mackay
July: Rupert, Haily, Rexbury, Buhl, Malad, Pocatello, Nampa
August: Weiser, Preston, Caldwell, Idaho Falls, Montpelier, Gooding, Burley, Filer
September: Jerome, Lewiston

IOWA

August: Sidney
September: Fort Madison

KANSAS

July: Topeka
August: Phillipsburg, Pretty Prairie, Lakin, Abilene
September: Dodge City

MINNESOTA
July: Walnut Grove

MISSOURI
September: Brookfield, St. Joseph

MONTANA
June: Deer Lodge
July: Livingston, Butte, Shelby, Lewiston
August: Great Falls, Billings, Sidney

NEBRASKA
June: Grand Isle
July: Mullen
August: Franklin, Burwell, Bladen, Broken Bow
September: Gordon, Omaha

NEVADA
June: Elko
July: Reno
August: Fallon

NEW MEXICO
June: Santa Rosa
July: Red River, Clayton, Cimarron, Grants, Santa Fe
August: Las Vegas, Artesia, Montainair
September: Silver City, Clovis, Springer, Farmington, Portales
October: Roswell

NORTH DAKOTA
July: Mandan, Sanish

OKLAHOMA
July: Shawnee, Hinton
August: Elgin, Ada, Chickasha, Vinita, Elk City

OREGON
June: Sheridan, Roseburg
July: Mollala, Klamath Falls, Yoncalla, Nyssa
August: Princeville, Redmond
September: Pendleton

SOUTH DAKOTA
June: Clear Lake, Pierre, St. Onge
July: Martin, Belle Fourche, Mobridge, Fort Pierre, Huron, Custer, Madison, Mission
August: Deadwood, White River, Rapid City, Faith
September: Rosebud, Sturgis

TEXAS
June: Gladewater, Burkburnett, Texarkana, Littlefield, San Saba, Lubbock
July: Amarillo, Clarksville, Pecos, Sulphur Springs, Big Springs
August: Rusk, Dublin

UTAH
July: Nephi
August: Logan

WASHINGTON
August: Cusick, Omak, Spokane
September: Walla Walla, Ellensberg, Puyallup

WISCONSIN
September: Milwaukee

WYOMING
June: Tie Siding
July: Cody, Lander, Sheridan, Cheyenne
August: Pinedale, Riverton, Douglas
September: Thermopolis, Evanston

CANADA (ALBERTA)
June: Edmonton, Lethbridge, MacLeod
July: High River, Medicine Hat, Claresholm, Calgary, Cardston

149

GLOSSARY OF COWBOY TERMS

MUCH HAS BEEN WRITTEN in recent years about the language of the American cowboy. Colorful, spirited "airin' of the lungs," as one cowhand put it, this jargon has done much to influence the development of the American language. Such terms as *hoodlum, buckaroo, hoose-gow* and *maverick* — once the exclusive property of the range rider — have now come to enrich and enliven the speech of all Americans.

Although this glossary defines dozens of these colorful terms. it makes no claim to completeness. Many of the most important words and phrases have been defined at such length in the body of the book that it seemed wisest — because of limitations of space — to omit them here.

Special thanks are due William Morris, editor of WORDS: *The New Dictionary* for his enthusiastic assistance in organizing this glossary.

albino *n*. A white or light cream-colored horse.

amble *v*. To move in an easy-going fashion whether on foot or horseback. "Let's amble over to the corral."

angoras *n. pl*. Goat-hide chaps.

Association saddle. Saddle adopted by the rodeo associations and required in all official contests. It is designed so that, as the riders say, "it gives the horse all the best of it."

axle grease. Butter.

bake *v*. To ride a horse until it becomes overheated.

band *n*. A group. Used only of horses, as "a band of horses." When referring to cattle, the cowboy uses "bunch."

bed roll. Roll containing tarpaulin, blankets, slicker and toilet articles, usually tied on the back of the saddle but sometimes carried in the bed wagon.

bed wagon. Wagon carrying bed rolls, stamping irons, etc., on roundup or trail drive.

blind bucker. A bronc which bucks aimlessly, esp. one which bucks right into a fence or other obstacle.

blizzard *n*. Severe snowstorm with sub-zero temperatures and driving gales.

blow a stirrup. To let the foot come out of the stirrup. In rodeo contests, this disqualifies the rider.

boil over. Pitching by an unbroken bronc when the buster tries to mount.

booger *n*. Any of many fears common to cattle.

bottom *n*. Endurance. "That bronc has plenty of bottom" means that he has good staying power.

brahma steer. Cross between Indian Brahma bull and Texas longhorn cattle, used in bulldogging contests.

brasada n. (Mexican) Brush country.

break *v*. To subdue and train a wild horse.

bronc *n*. A hard-pitching, unbroken horse. This term is not used after a horse has been sufficiently "gentled."

bronc riding. Now the feature event in rodeos, this probably developed from the natural rivalry of ranch hands, each eager to outdo the other in proving skill and endurance by riding unbroken horses.

brush country. Range covered with mesquite, greasewood, etc.

brush popper. A ranch hand in brush country.

buckaroo *n*. A cowboy — from the Spanish, *vaquero*.

bucking roll. Leather pad fastened to either side of the saddle fork to help rider to retain seat while breaking a bronc — not allowed in rodeo contests.

bulldogging. Rodeo event in which the unmounted contestant wrestles a steer to ground. Also called *steer wrestling*.

bunk house. Sleeping quarters on a ranch for cowhands.

caballero *n*. (Spanish-Mexican) Horseman.

cow n. Cattle, regardless of sex, are called "cows" by ranch hands.

cowpoke, cow puncher. Slang terms for *cowboy*.

cow whip. Whip, usually of braided leather and from 20 to 40 feet long, used instead of a lariat by hands on some Southern ranges.

coyote *n*. A prairie wolf. Also — used of a man — a low, sneaking wretch.

cutting horse. A horse specially trained to cut individual cows out of a herd.

dally *v*. In roping, to take a half-hitch around the saddle horn, using the leverage thus obtained to loosen or take up on the rope as the situation demands.

dogie *n*. A motherless calf, esp. one with a bloated belly.

drag rider. The hand who has to ride at the rear of the herd.

Dutch oven. A deep frying pan, usually three-footed, used to cook the cowhand's food over open fires. Often hot coals are heaped over the cover so cooking is done from both top and bottom.

earmark *n. & v*. Cut usually on the left ear of cattle, signifying ownership — usually supplementing burned brand.

The Cowboy and His Horse

equalizer *n.* A pistol or six-shooter — from the saying that a pistol makes all men equal.

fall back. A vicious mankilling horse which deliberately tries to rear so high he will fall back and crush his rider.

fence rider. A cowhand who checks range fences to keep them repaired.

fish *n.* Yellow oilskin slicker raincoat, so called from the trademark insignia.

gentle *v.* To tame an unbroken bronc.

git-up end. A horse's hind end.

honda *n.* A spliced eyelet or metal loop at the end of a rope used for making a loop.

hog belly. Salt pork.

hogtie *v.* To tie an animal, esp. cattle, by binding its hind legs and a front leg with a short rope.

hole up. To go into hiding.

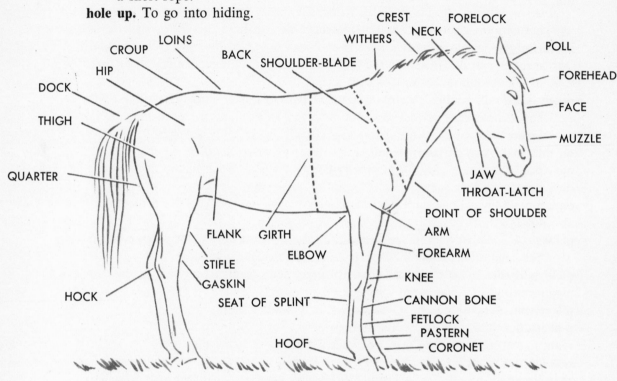

The Western Cow Horse

hood or **hoodlum** *n.* Driver of the bed wagon.

hoosegow *n.* (From Spanish *juzgado*) Jail.

Indian gentled. Said of a horse which has been very painstakingly broken in the Indian manner, esp. one which may be mounted from the right or "Indian" side.

Indian sign. A curse or hex.

lariat *n.* A rope, esp. one made of horsehair or grass. (From Spanish *la reata*.)

lasso *n.* A line or rope, esp. one used to rope calves and steers.

latigo *n.* The leather strap used to secure the saddle on the horse.

lead man. One of two riders who flank the lead point on a cattle drive.

lead steer. The steer which takes the lead in a trail drive.

Levis *n.* Trademarked name for a brand of dungarees or blue jeans favored by cowhands for their excellent wearing qualities.

152

line rider. Ranch hand who has to ride a prescribed route, checking on all conditions of land, cattle, etc.

loco *adj.* Crazy, foolish, "teched." From the *loco weed* which causes erratic behavior in cattle who graze on it.

makin's *n.* Loose tobacco and cigarette paper with which the oldtime cowboy used to "roll his own" cigarettes.

maverick *n.* Unbranded cattle.

mochila. A knapsack or, esp. on pony express saddles, a saddle pouch.

mossy horn. An old longhorn steer whose horns have become wrinkled.

muley. A steer without horns.

nester *n.* A homesteader or squatter.

night herd, night guard. The night watch over a cattle herd during roundup or trail drive. Usually two hands rode in opposite directions around the herd, exercising extreme caution so as not to arouse the cattle.

norther *n.* A particularly vicious kind of blizzard caused by gales from the north meeting warm winds from the Gulf of Mexico, resulting in sudden sharp drops in temperature.

notch in his tail. Said of a mankilling bronc who has, like gunfighters notching the handles of their six-shooters, put a "notch in his tail" for each man he has killed.

on the prod. Angry, fighting mad.

opry house. The top rail of the breaking corral where ranch hands sit and watch the "buster" at work.

outlaw *n.* A man or animal whose conduct places him outside the protection of the law.

paint *n.* A horse with large areas of white mingled with solid color. A showy horse but generally not too highly regarded for ranch work.

picking daisies. Said of a horseman who has been thrown.

piggin' string. The short, soft rope used to hogtie cattle.

pile driver. A horse which, in bucking, comes down with all four legs stiff.

pull leather. To grab the saddle horn when riding a bronc.

reata *n.* (Spanish) A rope, esp. one of rawhide.

remuda *n.* (Spanish) The string of horses herded in reserve during a roundup.

road brand. A brand, usually lightly burned in, use for all cattle involved in a particular trail drive, even though they may come from several ranches.

rowel *n.* The wheel of a spur.

run a brand. To brand cattle with a running iron; to adopt and use a particular brand.

saddle stiff. Nickname for cowboy.

scratching *adj.* With boots and spurs raking the forequarters of the horse. In bronc riding contests, under rodeo rules, each entrant must "come out scratching."

six-shooter *n.* Also **six-gun.** A revolver or pistol.

slow brand. An unrecorded brand, often used by rustlers.

spinner *n.* A bucking horse that rears up and backwards, instead of up and a forward plunge — one of the hardest buckers to ride.

spooky *adj.* Scared.

The Cowboy and His Horse

spread *n*. A ranch, usually including buildings, ranch hands and cattle.

Stetson *n*. Trade name for the broadbrimmed hat worn by most cowhands.

surcingle *n*. The belly band, esp. one used to hold the saddle on a horse.

tapadero *n*. (Spanish) Leather covering for stirrups to protect rider's feet from brush.

tarp, tarpaulin *n*. Heavy waterproof canvas.

tenderfoot *n*. An inexperienced person, esp. one newly arrived in the West.

trap corral. A corral especially designed to trap wild horses.

Tucson bed. Out of doors without shelter.

vaquero (Spanish) A cowhand. Used especially of Mexican cowboys.

vamoose *v*. (From Spanish *vamos*) To flee or get away fast.

waddy *n*. A cowboy. Originally an incompetent cowhand. Also, a rustler.

wet stock. Cattle smuggled by rustlers across the Rio Grande.

whitefaces *n*. Hereford cattle.

windies *n*. Cattle driven out of canyons and brush. So-called because both cattle and cowhorse are usually winded when the job is done.

wrangler *n*. Ranch hand who herds and tends the horses.

yearling *n*. A year-old calf or colt.

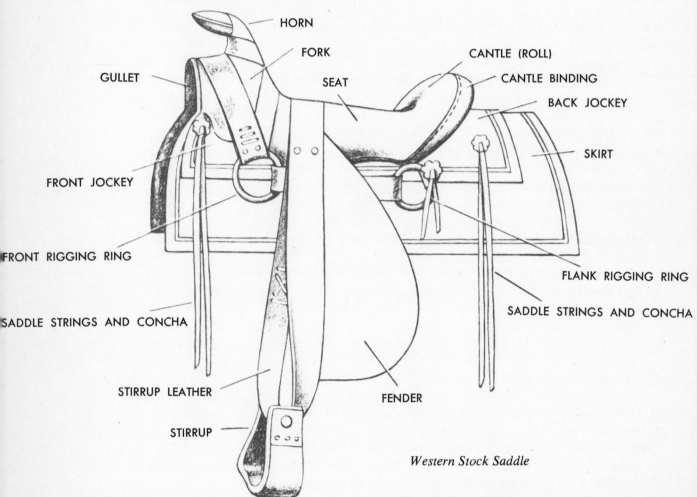

Western Stock Saddle

154

BIBLIOGRAPHY

FROM THE MANY HUNDREDS OF BOOKS written about the American cowboy and the opening of the West, these books have been chosen as the most interesting and authentic. Each book can be enthusiastically recommended to the reader seeking further information on any particular phase of Western life.

ADAMS, ANDY: *Log of a Cowboy,* Houghton, 1931

ALLEN, JULES VERNE: *Cowboy Lore,* Naylor, 1933

ARNOLD, OREN: *Sun In Your Eyes,* University of New Mexico Press, 1947
    and HALE, JOHN P.: *Hot Irons,* Macmillan, 1940

BOWMAN, JAMES CLOYD: *Pecos Bill: The Greatest Cowboy of All Time,* Whitman, 1937

BRANCH, EDWARD DOUGLAS: *The Cowboy and His Interpreters,* Appleton, 1926
    Hunting of the Buffalo, Appleton, 1929
    Westward: The Romance of the American Frontier, Appleton, 1930

CUNNINGHAM, EUGENE: *Triggernometry,* Caxton Printers, 1941

CUNNINGHAME, GRAHAM, R. B.: *Horses of the Conquest,* University of Oklahoma Press, 1949

DENHARDT, ROBERT M.: *Horse of the Americas,* University of Oklahoma Press, 1947

DOBIE, J. FRANK: *Apache Gold and Yaqui Silver,* Little, Brown, 1939
    Flavor of Texas, Dealey & Lowe (Texas), 1936
    Guide to Life and Literature of the Southwest, University Press in Dallas, 1943
    The Longhorns, Little, Brown, 1941
    On the Open Range, Southwest Press, 1931
    A Vaquero of the Brush Country, Little, Brown, 1943
    Voice of the Coyote, Little, Brown, 1950

GRANT, BRUCE: *The Cowboy Encyclopedia,* Rand McNally, 1951
    and SPINELLI, LARRY: *Leather Braiding,* Cornell Maritime, 1950

GRAUMONT, RAOUL, and HENSEL, JOHN: *Encyclopedia of Knots and Fancy Rope Work,* Cornell Maritime, 1942

GRINNELL, GEORGE BIRD: *Beyond the Old Frontier,* Scribner's, 1950
    The Fighting Cheyennes, Scribner's, 1915

HAFEN, LE ROY: *The Overland Mail, 1849-1869,* A. H. Clark (Ohio), 1926
and RISTER, C. C.: *Western America,* Prentice-Hall, 1941
HOUGH, EMERSON: *The Story of the Cowboy,* Grosset & Dunlap, 1925
The Story of the Outlaw, Grosset & Dunlap, 1925
HUNTER, J. MARVIN: *The Trail Drivers of Texas,* Cokesbury Press, 1927
JAMES, MARQUIS: *The Raven: The Life Story of Sam Houston,* Bobbs-Merrill, 1929
LOMAX, JOHN A.: *Songs of the Cattle Trail and Cow Camp,* Duell, Sloan & Pearce, 1950
and LOMAX, ALAN: *Cowboy Songs and Other Frontier Ballads,* Macmillan, 1948
MASON, BERNARD S.: *Roping,* A. S. Barnes, 1940
MORA, JOSEPH JACINTO: *Californios,* Doubleday, 1949
Trail Dust and Saddle Leather, Scribner's, 1946
MYERS, JOHN MYERS: *The Tombstone Story,* Grosset & Dunlap, 1951
PARKMAN, FRANCIS: *The Oregon Trail,* Modern Library, 1947
PERRY, GEORGE SESSIONS: *Roundup Time: A Collection of Southwestern Writing,* McGraw-Hill, 1943
Texas: A World in Itself, McGraw-Hill, 1942
RAINE, WILLIAM MACLEOD: *Famous Sheriffs and Western Outlaws,* Garden City, 1944
Guns of the Frontier, World, 1946
and BARNES, WILL C.: *Cattle,* Doubleday, Doran, 1930
REMINGTON, FREDERIC: *Crooked Trails,* Harper, 1923
Pony Tracks, Harper, 1923
ROLLINS, PHILIP ASHTON: *The Cowboy,* Scribner's, 1936
ROOSEVELT, THEODORE: *Stories of the Great West,* Appleton-Century, 1940
The Winning of the West, Putnam, 1920
RUSSELL, CHARLES M.: *Good Medicine,* Doubleday, 1929
Trails Plowed Under, Doubleday, 1941
SIRINGO, CHARLES A.: *Riata and Spurs,* Houghton Mifflin, 1931
Texas Cowboy, Sloane
SMITH, LAWRENCE BREESE: *Dude Ranches and Ponies,* Coward-McCann, 1936
SONNICHSEN, CHARLES L.: *Billy King's Tombstone,* Caxton Printers, 1942
Roy Bean — Law West of the Pecos, Macmillan, 1943
TWAIN, MARK: *Roughing It,* Harper, 1934
VESTAL, STANLEY: *Old Santa Fe Trail,* Duell, Sloan & Pearce, 1941
Short Grass Country, Duell, Sloan & Pearce, 1941
Sitting Bull, Houghton Mifflin, 1932
Warpath and Council Fire, Random House, 1948
WEBB, WALTER P.: *The Texas Rangers,* Houghton Mifflin, 1935
WELLMAN, PAUL I.: *Death on Horseback,* Lippincott, 1947
The Trampling Herd, Lippincott, 1939

The Cowboy and His Horse

INDEX

(NOTE: Italicized page numbers refer to illustrations.)

Abilene, Kansas, 37
Airplanes, *89*, 125
Apache Indians, 80
Austin, Stephen F., 28
Automobiles, 125

Barber shops, frontier, *39*
Bareback bronc riding,
   139, 141, *147*
Bedding down, 48
Bedrolls, 70
Bell ox, 26
Belts, chap, *103*
Bits, *98-9*
Blackfeet Indians, 131
Blankets, saddle, *101*
Blind bucker, 146
Blind irons, 78
Blizzards, *117*
"Bog riding," *70-71*
Boots, cowboy, 91, *97, 104*
Bowie knife, *23*
Brahma steers, 61, 87, 139, *140*
Branding, *73*
   modern methods, 126
Brands, early Southwest, *74*
   Egyptian, *76*
   maverick, *35*
   Mexican, *15, 25, 77*
   origin, 76
   purpose, 75
   reading, 81, *82-5*
   registering, 75
   road, 42, *44*
   Texan, *28*

Breaking bit, *99*
Breast collar, *100*
Bridles, ear, *100*
Broken Bow, Nebraska, 13
Bronc busting, *108-109*
Bronc riding, *133-8*
   bareback, 141, *147*
   saddle, *12, 128, 134, 145*
Bucking, types of, 146
Buffalo, *34-5*
Bulldogging, 141, *142*
"Bull nurses," 37
Bull riding, *see* Steer riding
Bull whackers, 131

Caballeros, 16
Calf roping, 143, *144*
Calgary Stampede, 132
California, cowboys in, *60*
   reins, *100*
   roundups, 66
Canadian Mounted Police, 132
Cantle, *95*
Catholic missions, *62*, 67
Cattle, brands, *82-5*
   dangers to, *116-117*
   drives, *see* Trail drives
   earmarks, *86*
   in Mexico, 17
   rustlers, 75
   in Texas, *20-21*
   on trail, 43-9
   trains, 37
   watering, 48

Cattlemen associations, 75
Chaps, *103-104*
Cheyenne, Wyoming, 132
Chileno bit, *99*
Chinese bits, *98*
Chinooks, 117
Chisholm Trail, map, *45*
   origin, 35-6
   stampede on, *56-7*
Chuck wagons, *46*, 70
Chute, leaving the, *134*
Cinches, saddle, *96*
Circle riders, *40-41*, 71
Civil War, 34-5
Clothes, cowboy, 21, 38
Clowns, 141
Collar, breast, *100*
Colt revolver, *23, 106*
Corrals, branding, 73
   breaking, 109
Cortez, 15, 76
Cowboy dances, *29*, 120-122
Cowboys, clothes, 21, 38
   daily range life, 114-119
   Mexican, *16*
   migratory, 74, 119
   modern, 88
   modern equipment, 90-107
   origin, *22*
   range tools, *107*
   Texan, 19-23
   trail clothes, 44
   wages, 38
   weapons, 22, *23, 106-107*

Cowgirls, in rodeos, 139
Coyotes, *48*
"Cricket," *98*
"Crow hop," 146
Cuffs, cowboy, *102*
Custer County Rodeo, 13
Cutters, 41, 73

Dallas, Texas, 134
Dally-hold roping, 92
Dances, cowboy, *29,* 120-122
"Dinner-plate" saddlehorn, *93*
Double-rigged saddle, *92*
Dude ranches, 127

Ear bridles, *100*
Earmarks, *86*
Egyptian brands, *76*
Equipment, cowboy, 90-107

Fence riding, *123*
Fences, introduction of, 61
Fiesta de los Vaqueros, La, 132
Flankers, 73
Folk songs, 30
Fort Benton, Montana, 130-131
Frontier Day celebration, 132

Get Yo' Little Sagehens Ready,
121
Gloves, cowboy, *102*
Gold rush, 67
Greek bits, *98*
Grizzly bears, 63, *64,* 115

"Half-breed" bit, *98*
Hats, cowboy, 90
"Healing," *69*
Hereford cattle, 61, 87
Hitson, Jess, 80
Hobble, *107*
Holsters, revolver, *106*
Hondas, *18, 102*
Horses, breaking, 110
    dangers to, 116
    equipment for, *92-105*
    pack, 101
    Spanish, 16
    in Texas, 23, *24*
Hydrophobia, 116

Indian gentling, 113
Indians, 59, 131, 132

as cowboys, 61-2
Irons, branding, 77

JA Ranch, 88
Jack-rabbit roping, *130-31*
Jayhawkers, 58

King Ranch, 88-9
Kyacks, *101*

Lariats, 18
    modern, *102*
Latigos, *96*
Line riders, 61
Longhorns, disappearance of, 61
    origin, 17
    in Texas, 19
    on trail, 43-9
Loose herding, 72

Madison Square Garden,
    135, 136
Magdalena driveway, 124
Maverick, Samuel A., 35
Mexico, cowboys in, 15-19
Miller, Henry, 67
Mossyhorns, 42
Mountain lions, 115, *116*
Mouthpieces, horse, *98-9*
"Mule ears," *104*
"Murder" steer, *79*
Mustangs, 23-4

Navajo Indians, 132
Night herding, *50-51*
Night-Herding Song, 52
Northers, *117*

Old Twisted Foot, 115
Operation Haylift, 125, *126*
Osage Indians, 59
Oxen, *63*

Pack saddle, *101*
Palo Pinto County, Texas, 27
Pecos, Texas, 130
Peeler, bronc, *111*
Picket, Bill, 141
Pick-up man, *12, 129*
Piegan Indians, 131
Piggin string, 138, 144
Pikes, Mexican, *17*
"Pile driver," 146
Prescott, Arizona, 132

Quirt, *110*

Racking bit, *99*
Railroads, 37, 39
Ranches, Texan, 87-9
Ranching, modern, 123
Range riding, 114-19
Range tools, *107*
Rattlesnakes, 116, *118*
Reatas, 17, *18*
Reins, *100*
Remudas, 46
"Reps," 59
Revolvers, *106*
"Riding the chuck line," 74
Rifle scabbard, *93*
Rifles, muzzle-loading, *23*
    Winchester, 107
Rigging, saddle, 95
River crossing, 49
Rodeo Cowboy Association, 139
Rodeos, Australian, 129
    eastern, 133-135
    old-time, 132
    origin, 31, 130
    prizes at, 130
    scoring in, 139-45
    unusual events in, 135
    world's championship, *136-137*
Romal, *100*
Ropes, *see* Lariats, Reatas
Roping saddle, 93
Roundups, modern, 69-72
    old-time, 40-42
Rowel spurs, *105*
Running irons, 77
Rustling, 75
    early, 58-9
    modern defenses against, 89

Saddle bronc riding, *12, 128, 134,*
    145
Saddles, blankets, *101*
    California, 63, *66, 67*
    fitting of, *94-5*
    Mexican, *19*
    modern, *92-3*
    pack, 101
    rigging, *95*
Saddle-tree measurements, *94*
Santa Barbara Mission, *62*

Santa Gertrudis cattle, 88
Sawbuck pack saddle, *101*
Scabbard, *93*
Shorthorns, 88
"Side winder," 146
Single-rigged saddle, *92*
Skunks, 116
Slow brands, 75, 77
Songs, cowboy, 29, 51, 52
Spade bits, *98-9*
Spaniards, in Mexico, 15
Split reins, *100*
"Spooky" cattle, *124*
Spring roundup, modern, 69-72
   old-time, 40-42
Spurs, 16, 92, *105*
   California, *61*
Square dances, 30, 120-22
Stamford, Texas, 134
Stampedes, 55-8
Stamp irons, 77, *78*
Steer decorating, 142

Steer riding, 139, *140*
Steer wrestling, *see* Bulldogging
Stetson hat, 91
Stirrups, *96*
Stock saddle, 93
Stockyards, 37
Stunt riding, 139
"Sunfishing," 146
"Sunning his moccasins," *133*
Surcingle, 141
"Swallowing," *12*
"Swapping ends," *14, 138,* 146
Sweet Betsy from Pike, 30, *32*

Tapaderos, *66, 67, 97*
Tarp, 70
Texas, independence of, 18
   modern ranches in, 87-9
   reins, *100*
Texas Rangers, 75
Tie-fast roping, 92
Tolliver, Lem, 27
Tomahawk, 59

Tompkins, Harry, 135
Tools, cowboy, 107
Trail drives, 26-8, 37, 43-9
   map, 45
   modern, 88, 124
Traps, grizzly bear, *115*
Tucson, Arizona, 132

United States Grazing Service,
   124

Vaqueros, Californian, 61
   Mexican, *16,* 17
Vent brands, 78

Waddies, *see* Cowboys
Winchester repeater, *107*
Winter ranges, *114-15*
Wolves, 115
World's Championship Rodeo,
   136-137

Yearlings, 74
Yellowbacks, 17, 40; *see also*
   Longhorns

My seat is in the saddle, and my saddle's in the sky;
And I'll quit punchin' cows in the sweet by and by.
          — *Song of the Chisholm Trail*

The text type used in this book
is Times New Roman, composed on the Linotype
by Linocraft, Inc., New York.
The chapter headings are Perpetua, hand set,
and the side headings are Bulmer, also hand set.
The book was printed in two-color offset lithography
by Reehl Litho, Inc., New York
and was bound by H. Wolff & Sons, New York.
The format is by A. P. Tedesco.